Singing Lessons for Little Singers

Very Young Beginner Series: Level B

Lesson and Work Book

By Greg Blankenbehler, M.A. Mus.

Illustrations by Erica Blankenbehler

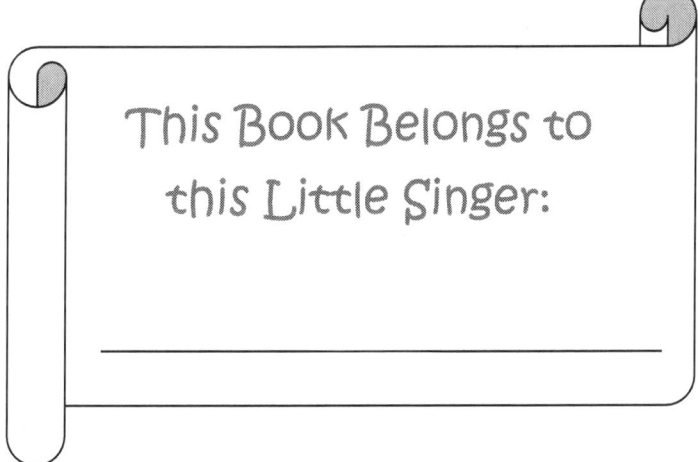

For more information on the **Singing Lesson for Little Singer™** method, visit us on the web at www.LittleSingers.info or email us at questions@littlesingers.info.

… Singing Lessons for Little Singers™ — Level B

Contents

To the Parents and *To the Teacher*..2
How to Use this Book..3
Level B Learning Objectives 4
      Technique Review *and* Windmills..5
      Body Scale Review *and* Singing High...6
Sameer the Singer 7-8
      Copy Cat is Back 9
      Rhythm Reading *and* Rhythm Cards..10
I've Got Rhythms 11-12
      The Body Scale: Re..13
      Melody Reading 14
The Grand Old Duke of York 15-16
      The Grand Old Duke of York Melody Descant *and* Percussion............................17-18
Kumbaya 19-20
      Kumbaya Melody and Harmony Descants 21
      Kumbaya Percussion 22
      Melody Reading: **By the Silver Moonlight** *and* **Mary Had a Little Lamb**.................23
      Sustained Notes Warm-up *and* Diction Practice 24
Twinkle Twinkle Little Star 25-26
      Twinkle, Twinkle Little Star Percussion 27
      Body Scale: Step Down to Ti 28
Go to the Circus 29-30
      Go to the Circus Percussion..31
      Body Scale: Leap Down to So 32
Frère Jacques/Are You Sleeping? 33-34
      Frère Jacques Piano 35
      Gallop Game 36
A-Hunting We Will Go 37-38
Level C Readiness Assessment 39
My Performance Record 40
Level B Certificate 41
Teacher Resources 42

Copyright 2014-15 by Gregory Blankenbehler. All rights reserved.

First Edition, Create Space (July 2015)

This book may not be photocopied or reproduced in part or whole in any form or manner without the express written permission of the author. All requests for permission or more information should be directed to questions@littlesingers.info.

Singing Lessons for Little Singers™ has been claimed in this enterprise as a trademark and cannot be used to advertise any product or service without the express permission of the author of this work.

Copyright 2015 Gregory Blankenbehler. All Rights Reserved. Photocopying Prohibited.

To the Parents...

Few things are more rewarding for a parent than watching musical talent blossom in their child's life. Musical training is an unparalleled mode of expression, achievement, and character development for young children. Recent research has debunked the old myths of inborn musical talent. We know today that every child's brain is born hard-wired to succeed in music. Unfortunately, most do not receive the early instruction needed to maximize that innate talent. Structured musical experiences in the early years are critical to developing the musical sensitivities and skills that will last a lifetime.

Though they surely still have a long way to go, you have no doubt begun to see your child's progress in musicianship (singing in tune and in time), as well as their confidence in performing. Your patient and diligent effort and encouragement will pay off over time as each lesson and home practice-play session is internalized. Again, I strongly encourage you to practice all assigned activities at home between lessons—that is where much of the musical growth takes place. As with all experiences in your child's life, every minute invested in music time will add up to create a wealth of skills and appreciation to enable a lifetime of music enjoyment.

Visit **www.LittleSingers.info/Parents** *for more information on the incredible benefits of studying music and what you can do as a parent to help your child succeed.*

To the Teacher...

Recent studies showing the early years to be crucial to musical-linguistic development conflict sharply with the traditional custom of waiting until late elementary to begin formal musical training. Indeed, respected childhood music experts Carl Orff, Zoltán Kodály, and Shinichi Suzuki began advocating for early music education nearly a century ago. **Singing Lessons for Little Singers™** Very Young Beginner Series focuses on the most natural musical expressions in children—singing and movement—while incorporating development in music literacy skills—aural skills and sight-reading—and building basic vocal and instrumental techniques—percussion and piano. This series was designed to be used with early elementary students (age 4-7), but would also be appropriate for older students needing more help with intonation, rhythm, and sight-reading. It was designed to be used in a small-group lesson format, but is also suitable for private instruction and adaptation to the classroom setting. Level B focuses on mastering the basic scale degrees (ear-training) with a big push towards rhythm and melody reading. The level also introduces percussion playing to aid in sight-reading development.

Singing Lessons for Little Singers™ has been carefully designed to provide teachers and their students with all the tools they need to succeed. *Teachers are highly encouraged to download and use the sing-along tracks, detailed lesson plans and other teacher support materials that are available in this book or online at* **www.LittleSingers.info/Teachers**. If you have any questions or comments, please feel free to email us at **questions@littlesingers.info** or leave a comment at **www.facebook.com/littlesingers**.

How to Use This Book...

Level B of **Singing Lessons for Little Singers**™ continues many of the structures and procedures first established in Level A. The songs and activities are designed to be used in lessons and home practice-play sessions to help students meet the "Level B Learning Objectives" listed on the following page.

Songs & Activities

The left teacher page and right parent/student page format for songs from Level A is mostly followed in Level B.

The parent/student page includes song lyrics, background story, and coloring-ready pictures to engage students. "Achievement Award" stars are to be colored in or replaced with a sticker when the task is completed.

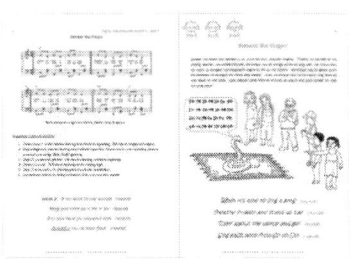

The teacher page includes simple written song accompaniments (piano/guitar) and suggested activities. More elaborate accompaniment tracks are available for free download on **LittleSingers.Info/Teachers**. Lesson plans are available in the Teacher Resource section, p. 55.

Body Scale

The body scale, first introduced in Level A, is continued and expanded in Level B to include new steps. It is an essential element of Level B. See p. 6 for additional instructions.

Copy Cat

The Copy Cat activity, also first introduced in Level A, is continued as an essential element of Level B. See p. 9 and p. 43 for instructions and melodic and rhythmic sequences to use for this activity.

Performing

As in Level A, both group and solo performances are an important element of Level B. Except in cases of extreme anxiety, students should be encouraged to participate in all Level B activities, including singing, instrument playing, movements, and games. Students should also regularly be given the opportunity to perform alone in lessons and at home. Record performances on p. 40.

Rhythm Reading

Rhythm reading, only briefly introduced in Level A, is a frequent and important activity in Level B.

In Level B, rhythms are written in a pictorial notation:

As in Level A, the notes should be read the following: quarter note="tah", quarter rest="shh:, eighth note pair="tee-tee", single eighth note="tee". Rhythms should be practiced with vocal syllables, clapping, and on percussion instruments.

Melody Reading

Melody reading, very briefly presented in Level A, is also a frequent and important activity in Level B. Preparatory to standard pitch notation, in Level B melodies are notated in solfege symbols on steps according to pitch height, often with a unique themed figure. (See p. 14.)

Instrument Playing

Instrument playing, only occasionally used in Level A, takes on a bigger role in Level B to promote better rhythm and musicianship skills. In addition to more frequent rhythm parts in songs and activities, piano playing is briefly introduced.

Copyright 2015 Gregory Blankenbehler. All Rights Reserved. Photocopying Prohibited.

Level B Learning Objectives:

Level B of **Singing Lessons for Little Singers™** *picks up where Level A left off, continuing development in the fundamentals of singing and musicianship. Students should first meet all Level A Learning Objectives before beginning Level B (see book or website for list). It is crucial that the teacher and parents regularly review these objectives to ensure that students are progressing towards their mastery in lessons and practice-play sessions.*

Ear Training

- ✓ Accurately repeat back short melodic sequences in "Copy Cat" (p. 43) using solfege labels with and without "Body Scale" gestures (p. 6) in low and high voice using the patterns in Levels A and B.
- ✓ Sing melody, harmony, and descant parts with solfege and lyrics together with others.
- ✓ Sing/Play all Level B songs and exercises with accurate pitches in multiple keys, high and low.

Rhythm

- ✓ Accurately repeat back short rhythmic sequences in "Copy Cat" (p. 43) using vocal rhythm syllables (p. 10), clapping, and simple percussion instruments using the rhythmic patterns in Levels A and B.
- ✓ Sing/Play all Level B songs and exercises with accurate rhythms.

Sight-reading/Singing

- ✓ Sight-sing all pictorially notated songs and exercises in Level B.
- ✓ Sight-play (clapping or on percussion instruments) and chant correct rhythm syllables for all pictorially-notated songs and rhythm exercises including rhythm cards (p. 46) in Level B.

Technique

- ✓ Demonstrate correct application of singing posture, belly breathing, high/low registers (p. 5), sustained support, and legato diction (p. 24).
- ✓ Sing comfortably in both high and low voice, from B below middle C to E an octave and a fourth above.
- ✓ Demonstrate simple percussion techniques (p. 22) in Level B songs and activities.
- ✓ Play "Frère Jacques" (p. 35) and possibly other Level A and B songs on piano using correct fingering.

Performance

- ✓ Perform all themed actions in Level B songs and activities.
- ✓ Perform several solos for parents/friends, and in class (p. 40).

Technique Review

Posture

In order to sing well, you must remember to stand up straight with your shoulders relaxed and back, and your head level. Make sure your feet are a little apart so you can stand strong!

Belly-Breathing

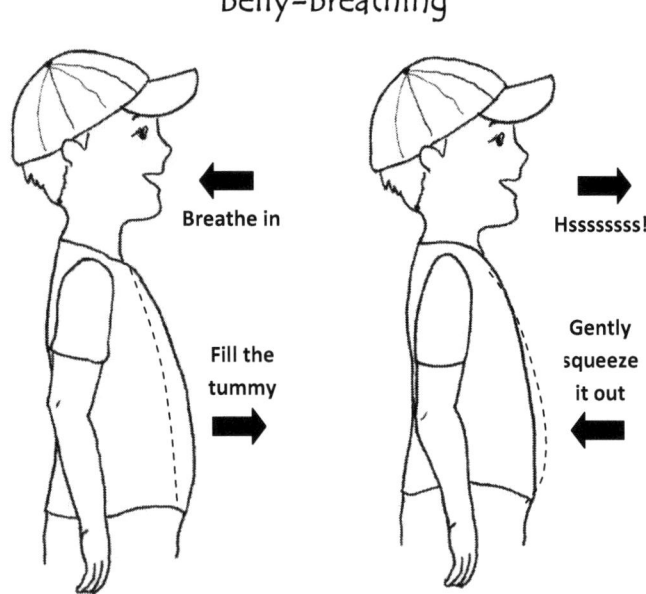

When you breathe in, make sure you open up your throat and fill up your lungs all the way down to your belly. Never lift your shoulders or chest! Then, when you hiss or sing, slowly squeeze the air out of your tummy from the bottom up.

Windmills

Beginning at the left hip, raise the right arm up in a wide circle over the head, out to the side, and down until it rests on the right thigh. Repeat with the left arm and then with both at the same time.

Try these fun variations:

1. Take a long, deep breath and then slowly hiss as you move your arms around, keeping the hissing steady until the arm(s) come to rest at your side.
2. Repeat with buzzing or "oo"ing, on a steady pitch.
3. Repeat with "whoo"ing or humming that raises and lowers in pitch according to the height of the hand movement.

The Body Scale – Low

In Level A we learned five different steps in the Body Scale: Do – Mi – Fa – So – La. (Pronounced "doh," "mee," "fah," "soh," "lah") Let's practice doing each motion as we sing up and down the steps of the scale that we know. (Begin Do on various pitches between C and E) Great!

Take a good look at the boys and girls on the steps above. They will help you learn how to read music later in this book. Color the step and the clothes of the child standing on it according to the color indicated below each step.

Singing High

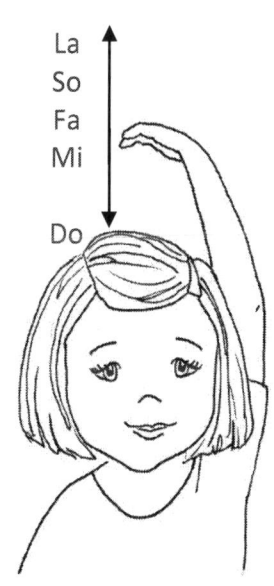

In Level A we also learned how to sing in our high voices. Let's sing some sirens beginning on very high notes and dropping down. While doing this, sweep your hand slowly forward over your head and down with the pitch. Now try sliding up into high voice and then back down. Great! Now let's try singing the Body Scale in high voice. (La-So-Fa-Mi-Do, use F and higher for Do)

Teacher Notes: "Body Scale" gestures are very useful in helping singers correctly place and track pitches and solfege syllables. They also prepare students to follow the ups and downs of notated pitches. Care should be taken, however, not to overload students' thinking during songs and activities. "Body Scale" gestures should typically be used for aural practice activities such as "Copy Cat" (p. 9) and not during sight-singing (beginning p. 14). Do use "Copy Cat" throughout Level B to practice singing correct intervals.

Sameer the Singer

Each two-measure phrase is sung twice: first by leader, then by group.

Suggested Order of Activities

1. Chant Verse 1 words: teacher leading and students repeating. Talk about singing techniques.
2. Sing solfege only: teacher leading and students repeating. Memorize by rote, repeating phrases over and over using "Body Scale" gestures. (See next page)
3. Sing V1 (words and pitches) with teacher leading, students repeating.
4. Chant V2 words. Talk about and practice techniques for singing high.
5. Sing V2 in key of F or G (starting pitch C or D above middle C).
6. Let students take turns being the leader while everyone else repeats.

Verse 2: *If you want to sing up high*   (repeat)

Hang your voice up in the in sky   (repeat)

O'er your head you sing each note   (repeat)

Beautif'ly you let them float   (repeat)

Sameer the Singer

Sameer the snake has learned a lot since he first started singing. Thanks to the help of his singing teacher, the snake-charmer, he knows lots of things to do to sing well. He knows how to stand up straight and breathe in deeply to fill up his tummy. He knows how to gently push his stomach in to make his voice sing steady. And, he knows how to correctly sing most of the notes of the scale. Now people come from all around to watch and copy Sameer so they can sing better.

So Mi So Mi So La So
So Mi Do Mi So Mi Do
So Fa Mi Fa So Fa Mi
So Fa Mi Re Do Do Do

When it's time to sing a song (repeat)

Breathe in deep and stand up tall (repeat)

Think about the words and go! (repeat)

Sing each note from So to Do (repeat)

Copyright 2015 Gregory Blankenbehler. All Rights Reserved. Photocopying Prohibited.

Copy Cat is Back

Let's play the "Copy Cat" game we learned in Level A. Remember, first I sing a phrase while you listen, then you sing it back to me exactly the way that I did it.

Teacher's Note: "Copy Cat" was introduced in Level A as a crucial activity for developing rhythm and intonation skills. See p. 43 for instructions and a complete list of melodies and rhythms to use for Level B.

Rhythm Reading

Now we're going to practice reading rhythms. All you have to do is point at each picture and say the rhythm syllables to a steady beat.

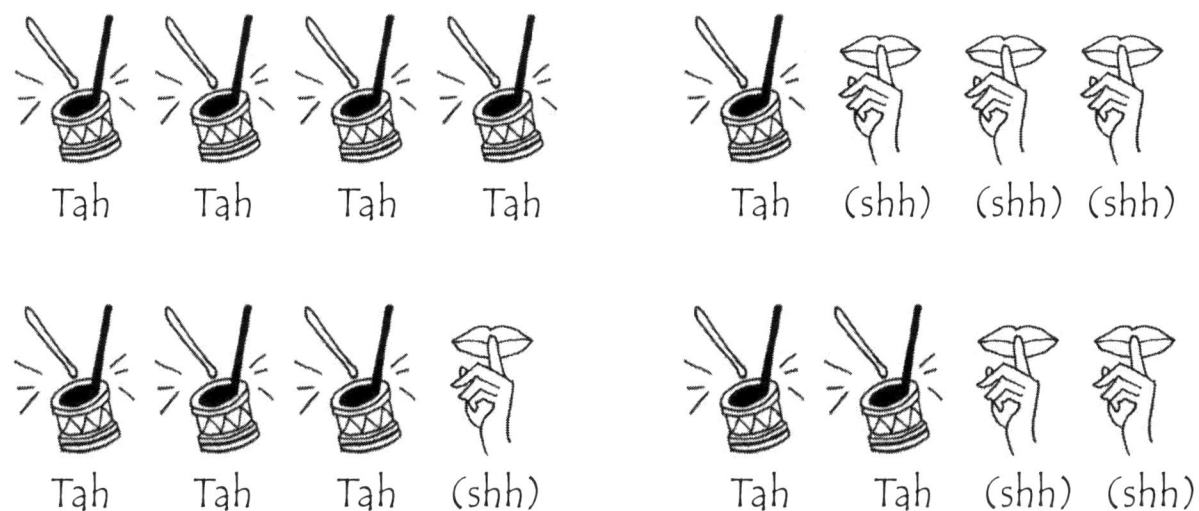

Great! Now let's try just looking at each rhythm and clapping them.

Rhythm Cards

Now let's play with rhythm cards. I'm going to make a stack of cards face down over here. As I turn over each card, point and say each rhythm in a steady beat.

Now try just looking at and clapping each rhythm to the beat.

Teacher's Note: See p. 46 for instructions and rhythm cards.

I've Got Rhythms

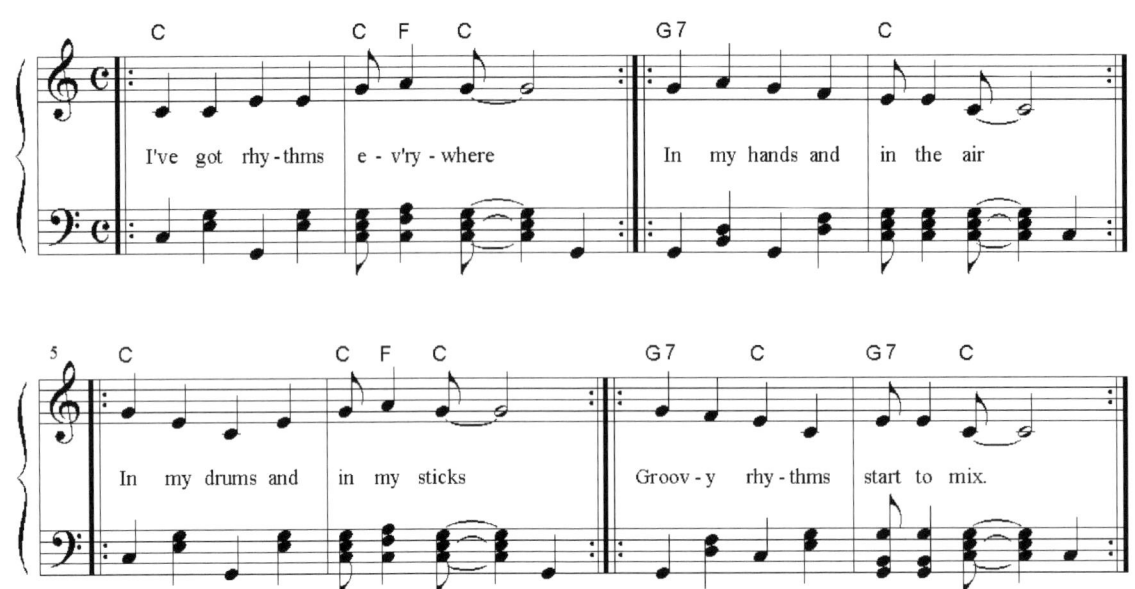

Suggested Order of Activities

1. Chant lyrics in rhythm. (Don't worry about doing rhythmic syllables for syncopated rhythm.)
2. Sing solfege in rhythm.
3. Sing song, followed by the four "Set 1" rhythm cards (see p. 46) along to the beat, with 4-count pause between each.

    Example:

    Measures 1-2/Card 1: Tah Tah Tah Tah – (rest 4 counts)
    Measures 3-4/Card 2: Tah Tah (shh) (shh) – (rest 4 counts)
    Measures 5-6/Card 3: Tah (shh) (shh) (shh) – (rest 4 counts)
    Measures 7-8/Card 4: Tah (shh) (shh) (shh) – (rest 4 counts)

4. Perform rhythms with clapping or percussion instruments.
5. Use rhythm cards from sets 2-4. Omit 4 counts of rest and mix sets as skills improve.

    Example:

    Measure 1/Card 1: Tah Tah Tah Tah – Measure 2/Card 2: Ti-Ti Ti-Ti Tah Tah
    Measure 3/Card 3: Tah Tah (shh) (shh) – Measure 4/Card 4: Tah Tah Ti-Ti Tah
    Measures 5/Card 5: Tah (shh) (shh) (shh) – Measure 6/Card 6: Ti-Ti Tah Tah Tah
    Measure 7/Card 7: Tah (shh) (shh) (shh) – Measure 8/Card 8: Tah Ti-Ti Tah Tah

I've Got Rhythms

The kittens love to visit their uncle Beatcat. It seems like there is always a jam session going on at his house. Whether singing, chanting, or playing on sticks, Beatcat always plays the coolest rhythms.

I've got rhythms everywhere

In my hands and in the air

In my drums and in my sticks

Groovy rhythms start to mix

(Sing rhythm cards to the beat)

Copyright 2015 Gregory Blankenbehler. All Rights Reserved. Photocopying Prohibited.

The Body Scale: Re

Now we are going to add another note onto our body scale. Re (pronounced "ray") is between Do and Mi, on our hips. You can sing it when you are going up from Do like this: "Do – Re – Mi," or going down like this: "Mi – Re – Do." Let's try going all the way up from Do to So. Wonderful! Now let's try them in high voice!

Color the "Do" boy and his step red, the "Re" girl orange, and the "Mi" girl yellow!

Try these fun copycat phrases! (See p. 43 for more copycat phrases)

𝄞 Do Do Re Re Mi Mi Mi

𝄞 So Fa Mi (Shh) Mi Re Do

𝄞 Do Re Mi Re Do Do Do

𝄞 Do Re Mi (Shh) Mi Fa So

𝄞 So La So Fa Mi Re Do

Copyright 2015 Gregory Blankenbehler. All Rights Reserved. Photocopying Prohibited.

Melody Reading

You have been doing so wonderfully at singing your notes! Now we're going to start learning to read them. Point at the boy that is standing next to the music symbol (𝄞) below and sing the note he is holding (Do). Then, point to the girl next to him and sing her note (Re). Then move to the girl next to her and sing her note (Mi). Great! Now try all three in a row. Wonderful! Now try another line of notes.

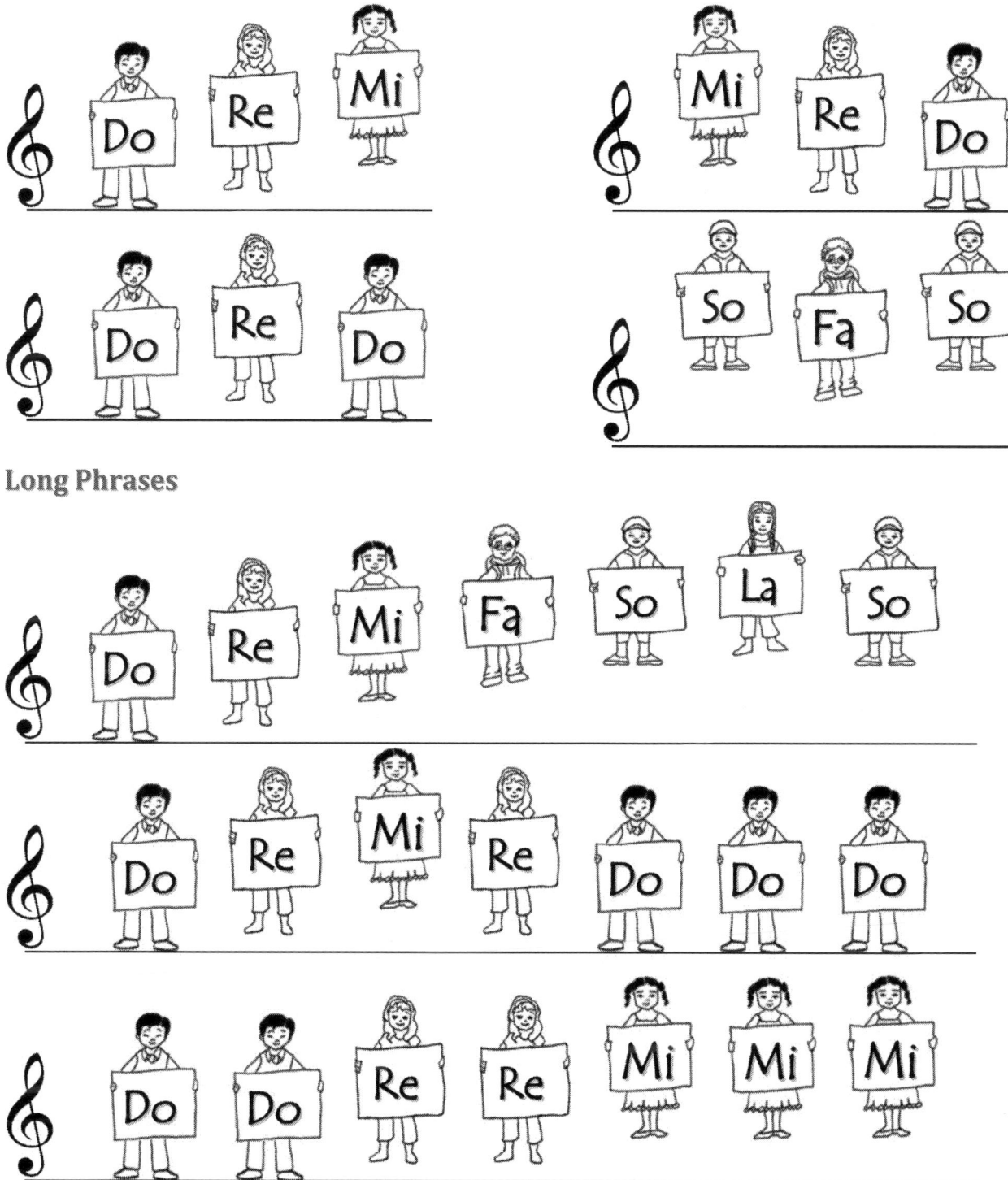

Long Phrases

The Grand Old Duke of York

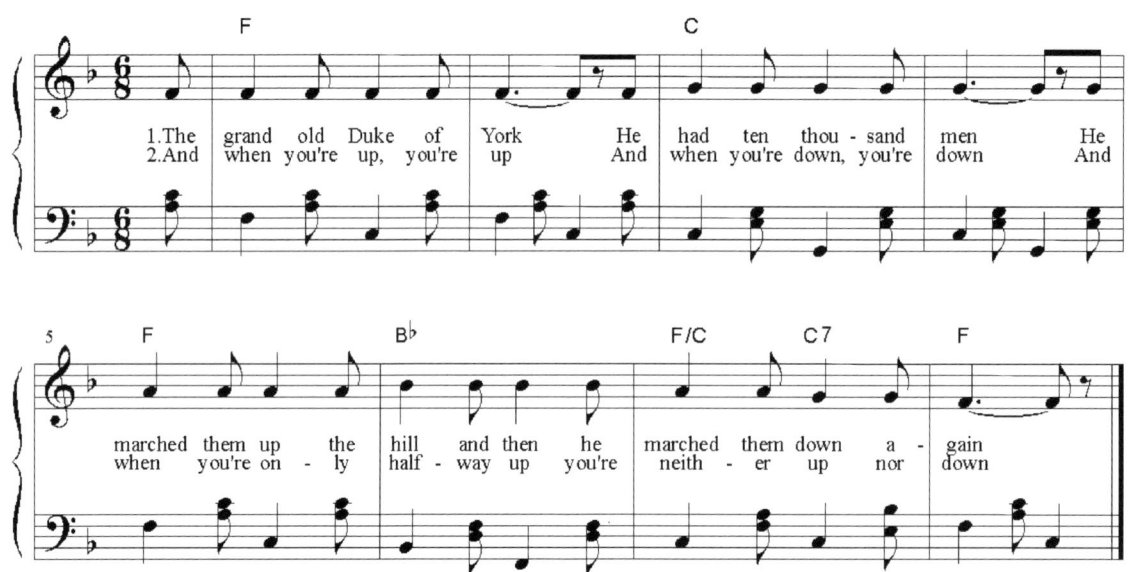

Suggested Order of Activities

1. Learn words and melody by ear. (Take care to teach the melody variant taught here! – See note below)
2. Play "Follow the Leader" while singing song. (Eg. March around room, stand up and sit down, etc.)
3. Add body-scale actions while marching to song:

...grand old Duke...	hands on knees, hunched over
...had 10,000 men...	hands on hips
...marched them...	point to chest
...hill and then...	hands on shoulders
...marched them...	point to chest
...down a-...	hands on hips
...-gain...	hands on knees, hunched over

4. Point and sing descant melody (in solfege) on page 17-18. Color in children according to p. 6.
5. Point and say percussion part. Look and play percussion part (clapping, thumping, sticks, drums, etc.)
6. Combine melody, descant, and rhythm parts.

Note on Song: There are two melodies to which this song is commonly sung. The simpler of the two was chosen here to aid early sight-reading (p. 17-18). Incidentally, the second melody is used in Level B for "A-Hunting We Will Go" (p. 38), which is also commonly sung using either melody.

The story described on the next page is completely fictional. There is little agreement among historians as to which person or event this folk song originally referred.

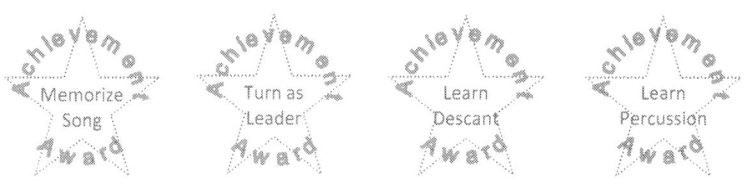

The Grand Old Duke of York

Many years ago, the Duke of York was the general of a huge army. It was his job to get his soldiers to walk the long distance from the city of York to London. In order to make their long journey more fun, the Duke of York would sing a song as they marched up and down the many hills in their path.

The grand old Duke of York
He had ten thousand men
He marched them up the hill
And then he marched them down again

And when you're up, you're up
And when you're down, you're down
And when you're only half-way up
You're neither up nor down

Copyright 2015 Gregory Blankenbehler. All Rights Reserved. Photocopying Prohibited.

Grand Old Duke of York – **Melody Descant**

Grand Old Duke of York – **Percussion**

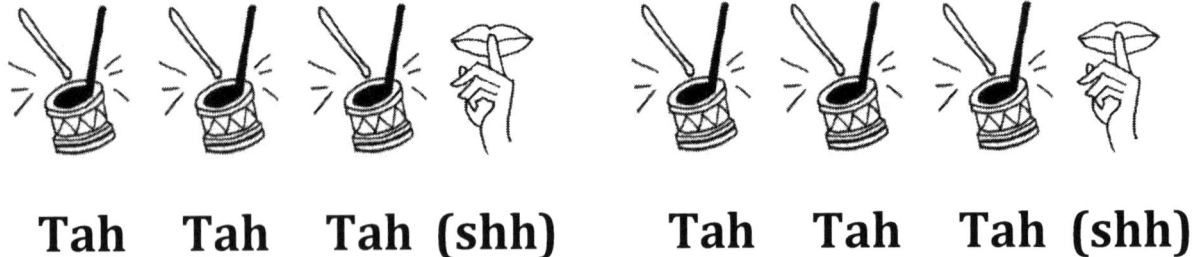

Teacher's Note - Descant: This descant is a simplification of the melody to aid sight reading. Begin teaching using "point and sing" in rhythm (hyphen indicates half note). Later, have students follow notes with their eyes while singing and doing "Body Scale" motions. This descant can also be sung by a small group while the rest sings the melody.

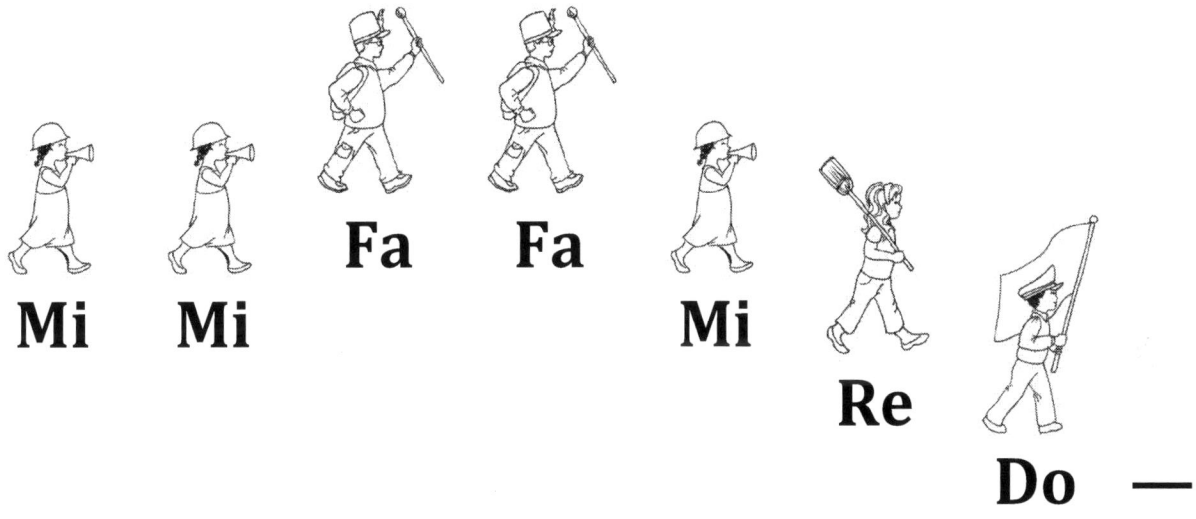

Mi Mi Fa Fa Mi Re Do —

Tah Tah Tah Tah Tah Tah Tah (shh)

Teacher's Note - Percussion: This percussion part is the same rhythm as the descant, except quarter rests are used where the descant uses half notes. Begin teaching using "point and say" with a steady beat. Then, have students follow with their eyes as they clap or use rhythm sticks. Finally, choosing a small group to play percussion part on drums while the rest sings would be quite effective.

Kumbaya

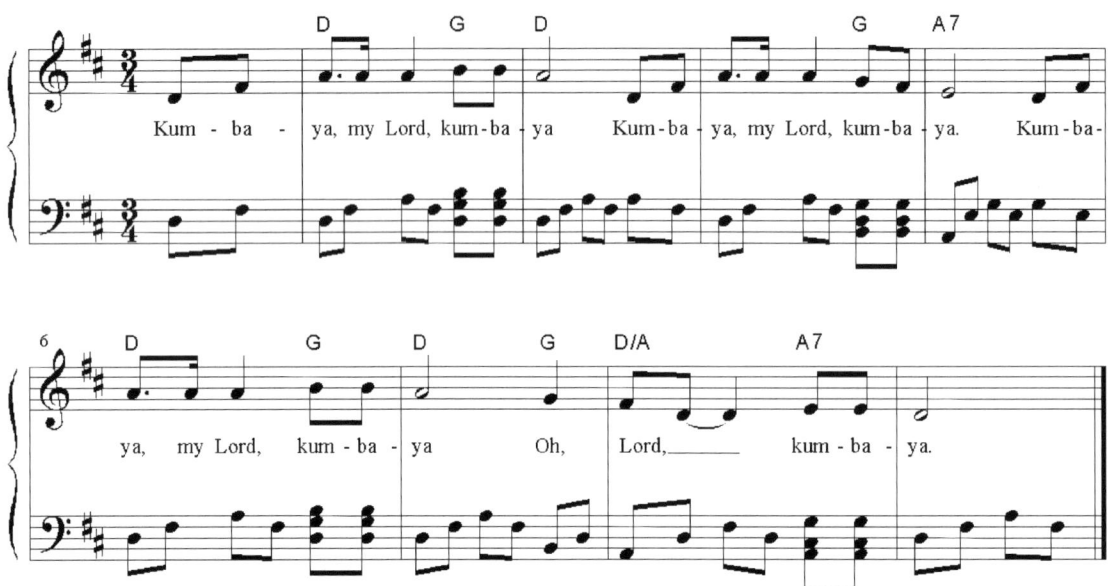

Suggested Order of Activities

1. Sing melody with words (pretend to be camping, singing around a campfire).
2. Sight-read percussion part (p. 22)
3. Sight-read pictorial melody in solfege (p. 21) Color in the children according to p. 6.
4. Students take turns making up new actions for additional verses. (eg. "Someone's *laughing* Lord, kumbaya.")
5. Sight-read harmony part. (p. 21)
6. Try performing with different groups on melody, harmony, and percussion parts.

Note on Song: The repeated phrase "Kum ba ya" (pronounced "koom-buy-yah") is widely considered to be an African-American creole variation of the English phrase "Come by here," though its origin is unknown.

Despite one composer claiming to have written this song around 1936, earlier recorded variations of the song dating back into the 1920's exist that it prove it was a common folk song among African-Americans in the southeastern United States. (See Library of Congress investigation: S. Winick, "The World's First Kumbaya Moment," *American Folklife Center News* [Library of Congress] 32, no. 3-4 (2010): 3-10.)

While "Kumbaya" is nowadays often ridiculed (particularly in politics) for its perceived message of *naiveté*, the actual song lyrics express none of the negative connotations it has been given in recent years. The song's simple and yet elegant melody, along with the ease with which it allows the creation beautiful harmonies and creative verse additions, makes it a particular treasure among traditional American folk songs.

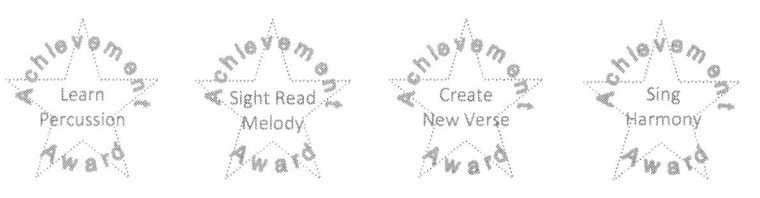

Kumbaya

It is so much fun to go camping! First, you pack up all your gear and drive to the forest. Then, you set up your tent and roll out your sleeping bag. Next, you cook a delicious camping meal on a portable gas stove. When it starts getting dark and cold, you build a campfire and sing songs with your friends. After roasting s'mores over the fire, you go to your tent and curl up for a nice, cozy sleep. I can't wait for all the fun we'll have tomorrow!

Kumbaya, my Lord, kumbaya (3x)
Oh, Lord, kumbaya

Someone's singing*, Lord, kumbaya (3x)
Oh, Lord, Kumbaya

(*Substitute new actions for repeated verses)

Kumbaya – **Melody**

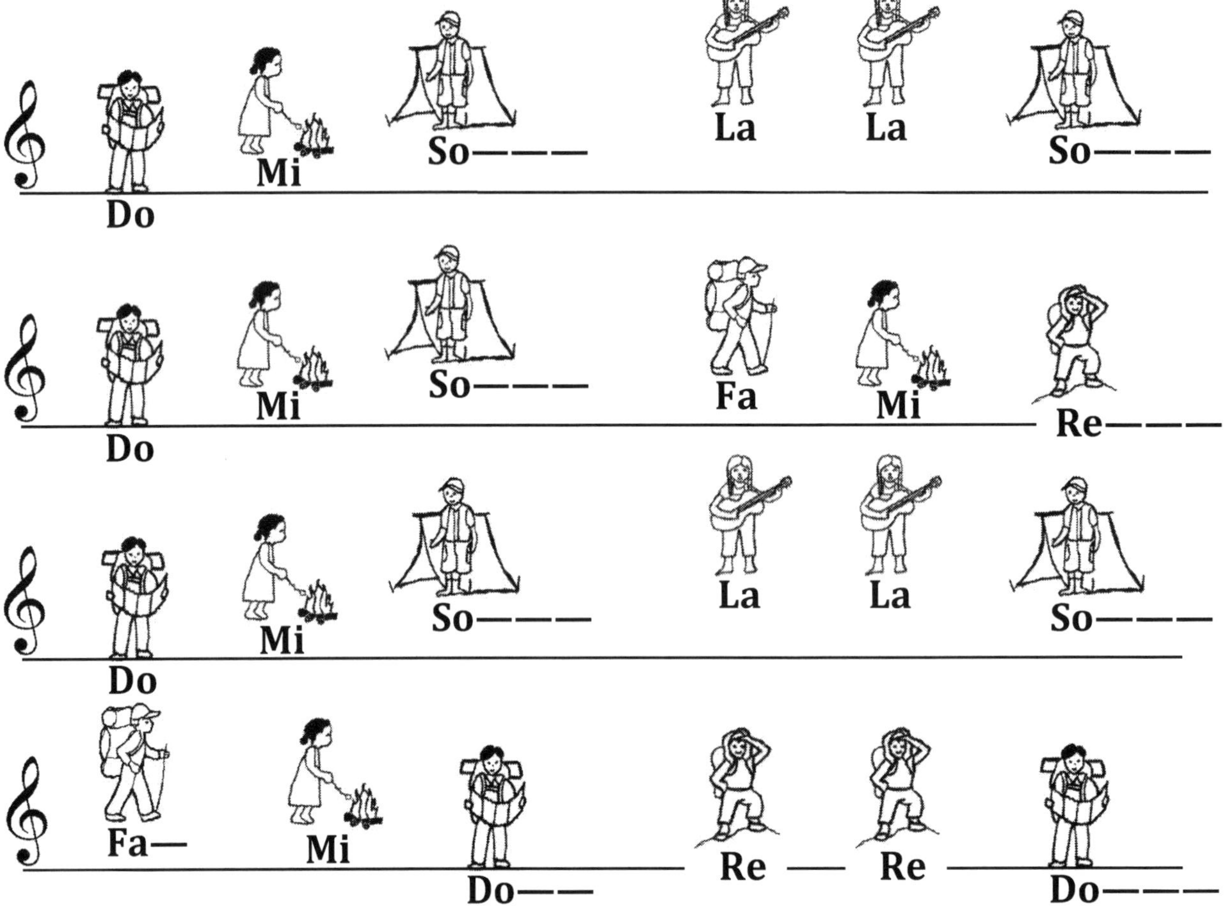

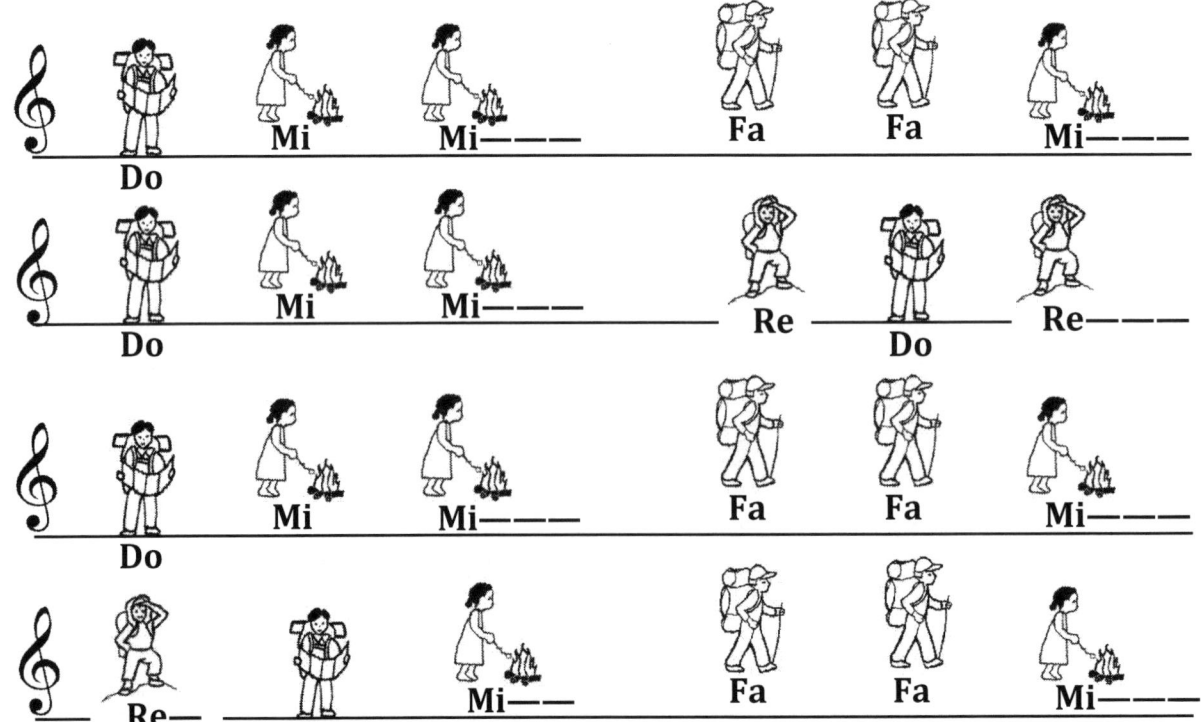

Kumbaya – **Harmony**

Kumbaya – Percussion

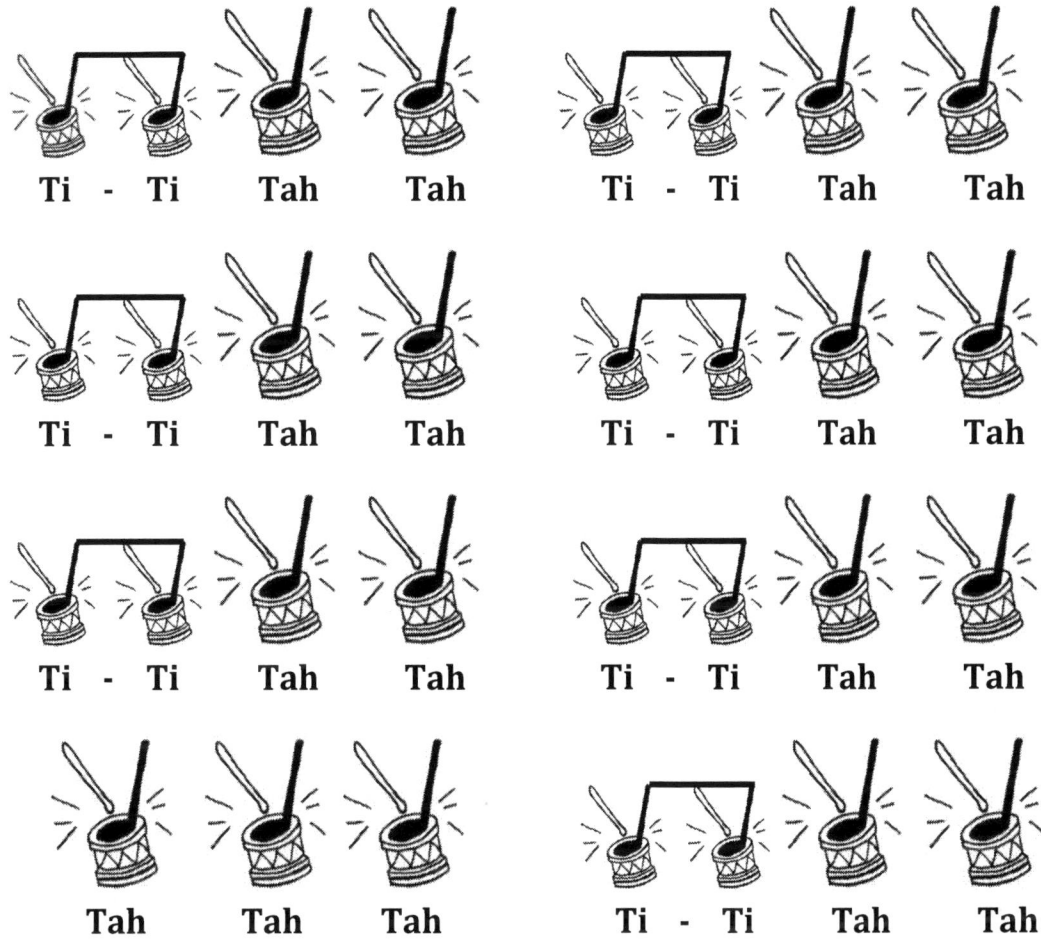

Teacher's Note: In addition to clapping, many rhythms in this book would be very effective played on a drum (or palms slapping knees, if drums are not available). It is suggested that pairs of eight notes be played "right hand – left hand," and that quarter notes be played with only the right hand. The same technique should also be used in other songs with pairs of eight notes. ("Rhythm Reading" p. 10, "Go to the Circus" p. 31.)

Example:

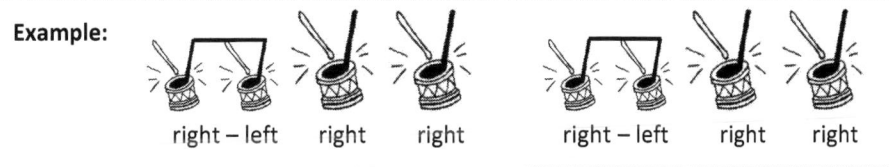

6/8 "Gallop" rhythms are more comfortably played "right hand – left hand."
("Gallop" p. 36, "A-Hunting We Will Go p. 38)

Example:

Copyright 2015 Gregory Blankenbehler. All Rights Reserved. Photocopying Prohibited.

Melody Reading: By the Silver Moonlight

By the silver moonlight; My dear friend Pierrot; Lend me please your pen so; I can write a note

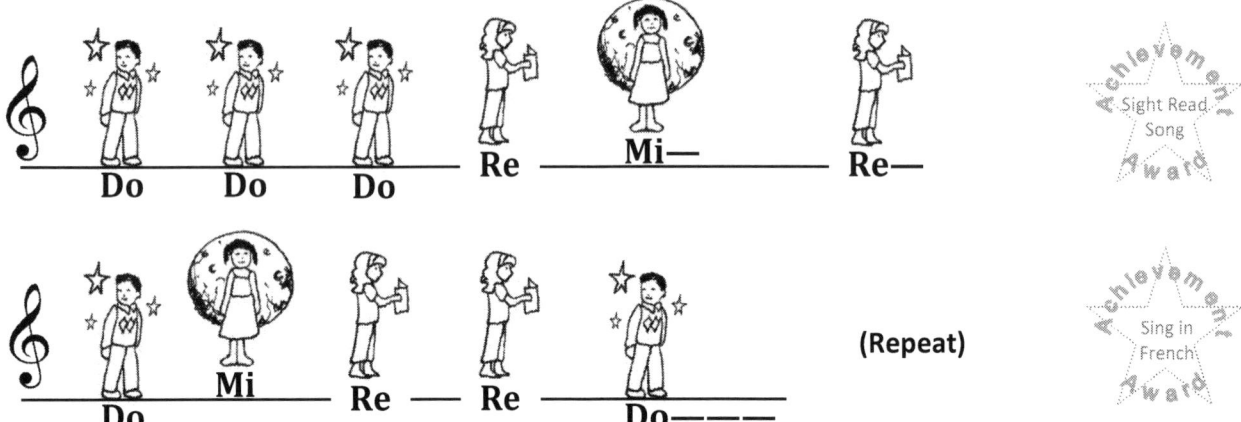

French words: *Au clair de la lune; Mon ami Pierrot; Prête-moi ta plume; Pour écrire un mot*
(oh claire duh lah loon-uh; mahn ah-mee pyair-oh; prett-uh mwah tah ploom-uh; poor ay-creer uh moh)

Melody Reading: Mary Had a Little Lamb

Mary had a little lamb; Little lamb, little lamb; Mary had a little lamb; It's fleece was white as snow.

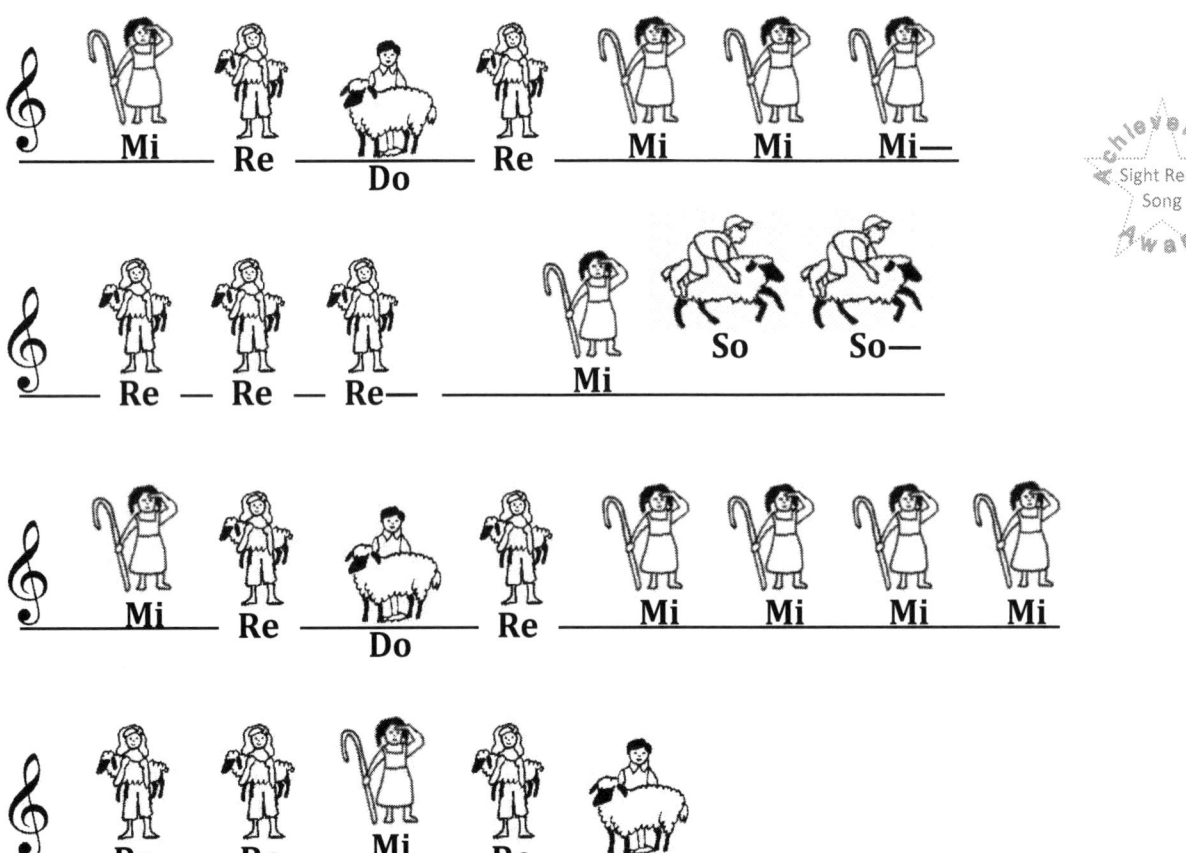

Sustained Notes Warm-up

Imagine that you were a squirrel running on a telephone line. As you run you sing "too!" Every time you reach a telephone pole, you quickly hop over it, start a crisp, new "too" and keep on running down the line, stretching the "oo" out to the next pole. How smoothly can you hop over those telephone poles? For more challenge, try singing a different solfege note after each pole!

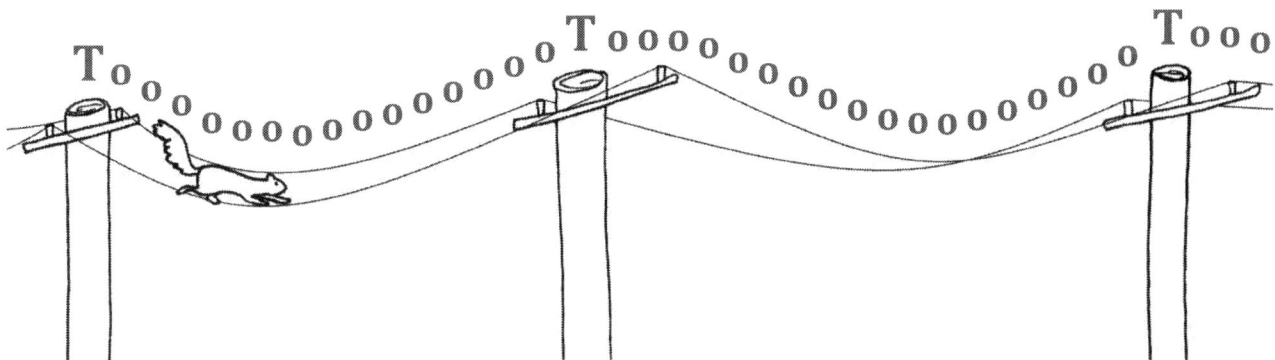

Diction Practice

When we talk, our words are short and crisp, but when we sing we need to stretch the vowels out to connect with the next word.

Practice talking the following phrase with short, crisp consonants and no sustained vowels: **(staccato)**

Ma   ry   had   a   lit   tle   lamb,

It's   fleece   was   white   as   snow.

Now practice singing it with crisp consonants, but adding long, sustained vowels between: **(legato)**

Ma-----------ry-----------ha-----------da-----------li-----------ttle-----------la-----mb, (breath)

I-----------t's flee-----------ce wa-----------s whi-----------te a-----------s snow.

Great! Now let's try it on some of our other songs.

Twinkle, Twinkle Little Star

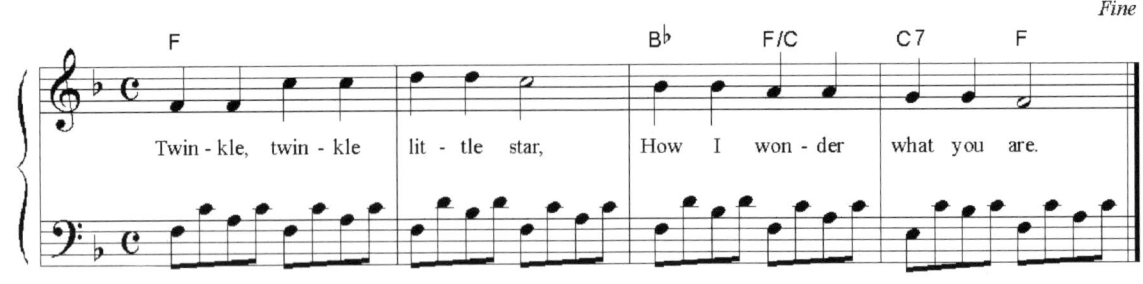

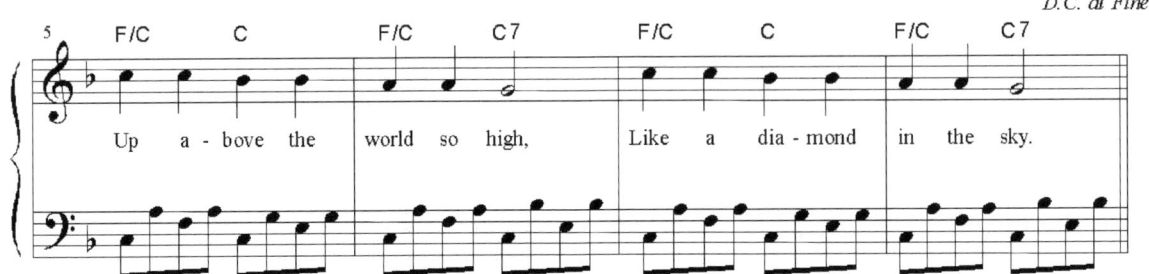

Suggested Order of Activities

1. Sight-read percussion part (p. 27).
2. Sight-read pictorial melody in solfege. (p. 26) Color in the children according to p. 6.
3. Sing melody with words.

    Add these actions, if desired:

Twinkle, twinkle...	hold up hands and open and close to the beat
How I wonder...	shrug shoulders and hold out open hands
Up above...	point up
Like a diamond...	hold hands high above head and make a diamond with pointers and thumbs
Twinkle, twinkle...	hold up hands and open and close to the beat
How I wonder...	shrug shoulders and hold out open hands

4. Combine melody and percussion. Sing additional verses together.
5. Students take turns singing additional verses solo, with everyone joining in for the final two (italics) lines.

Twinkle, Twinkle Little Star

There is something magical about the stars. Soaring high above the ground, each star shares its own light with everyone on the earth. You can be like a star when you stand up in front of your friends and family to share your music talents.

(Sing first and second lines again)

Twinkle, Twinkle Little Star – **Percussion**

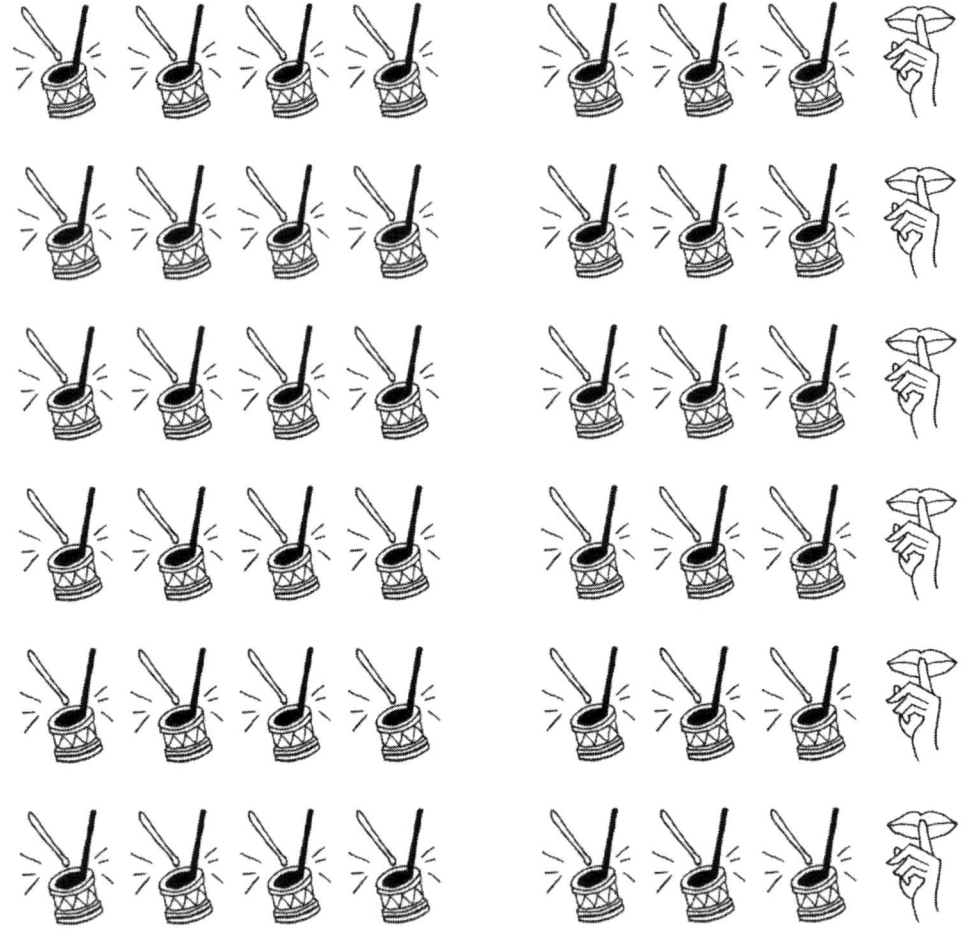

When the blazing sun is gone,
When he nothing shines upon,
Then you show your little light,
Twinkle, twinkle, all the night.
Twinkle, twinkle, little star,
How I wonder what you are.

Then the traveller in the dark,
Thanks you for your tiny spark,
He could not see where to go,
If you did not twinkle so.
Twinkle, twinkle, little star,
How I wonder what you are.

In the dark blue sky you keep,
Often through my curtains peep,
For you never shut your eye,
'Till the sun is in the sky.
Twinkle, twinkle, little star,
How I wonder what you are.

As your bright and tiny spark,
Lights the traveller in the dark.
Though I know not what you are,
Twinkle, twinkle, little star.
Twinkle, twinkle, little star,
How I wonder what you are.

Body Scale: Step Down to Ti

Did you know there is a note on the body scale below Do? It's called Ti **(pronounced "tee")** and you can make the gesture by taking your hands off your knees and pointing down. Try starting on Do, stepping down to Ti, and then back up to Do. Wonderful! Now let's try it starting on a higher Do!

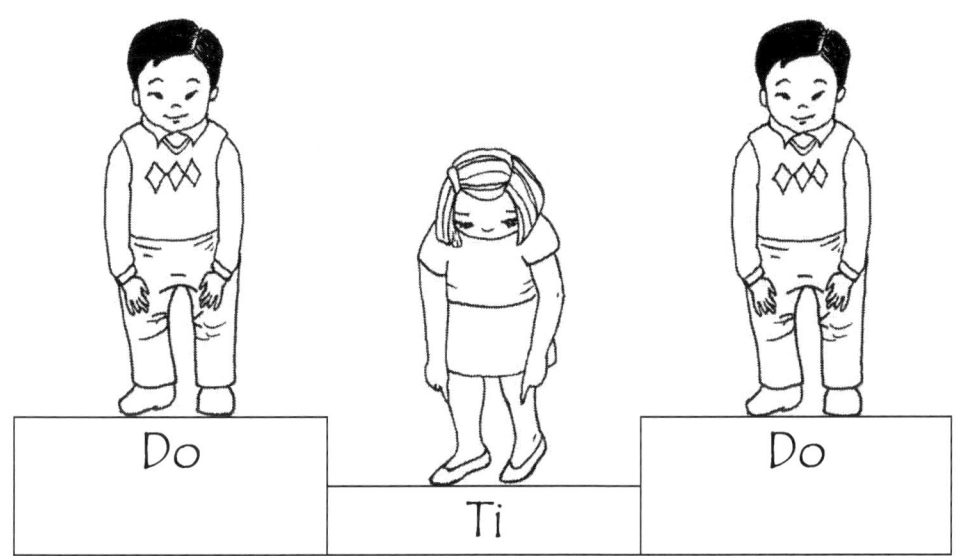

Color the "Do" boy red, the "Ti" girl pink!

Try these fun copycat phrases! **(See p. 43 for more copycat phrases)**

𝄞 Do Ti Do (Shh) Do Ti Do

𝄞 Do Re Mi Re Do Ti Do

𝄞 Do Ti Do Re Mi Fa So

𝄞 Do Mi So Mi Do Ti Do

𝄞 So Fa Mi Re Do Ti Do

Go to the Circus

Suggested Order of Activities

1. Complete beaming activity and sight-read percussion part. (p. 31)
2. Sight-read pictorial melody in solfege. (p. 30)
3. Sing melody with words. (Add motions, if desired.)
4. Game: Choose a circus performer to be as you sing the song and act out that part.

   Examples:
   a. A clown doing silly things
   b. An acrobat doing handstands and tricks
   c. A daredevil riding around on a motorcycle
   d. A lion tamer directing lions to do tricks
   e. A muscle-man lifting heavy weights
   f. An emcee welcoming everyone to the show

5. Combine melody and percussion.

Go to the Circus

I love it when the circus comes to town! There are so many fun things to see: Outrageously dressed clowns doing silly things; Elephants and lions balancing and doing tricks; Acrobats flipping and flying through the air on swings; Muscly men lifting heavy weights. What an exciting show they put on for us!

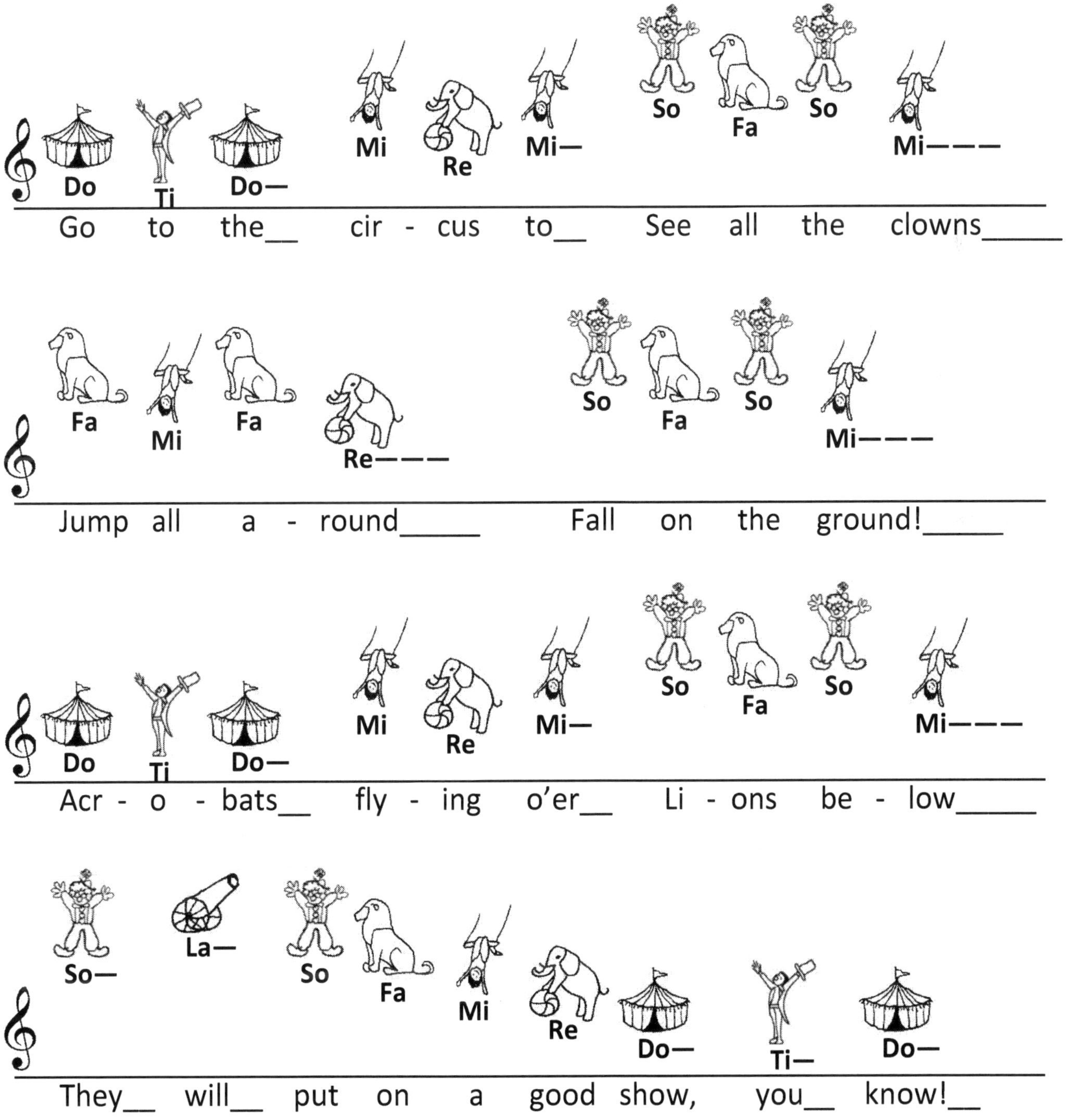

Do Ti Do— Mi Re Mi— So Fa So Mi———
Go to the__ cir - cus to__ See all the clowns____

Fa Mi Fa Re——— So Fa So Mi———
Jump all a - round____ Fall on the ground!____

Do Ti Do— Mi Re Mi— So Fa So Mi———
Acr - o - bats__ fly - ing o'er__ Li - ons be - low____

So— La— So Fa Mi Re Do— Ti— Do—
They__ will__ put on a good show, you__ know!__

Copyright 2015 Gregory Blankenbehler. All Rights Reserved. Photocopying Prohibited.

Go to the Circus – Percussion

Connect the poles on the small drums. Leave the poles on the big drums bare.

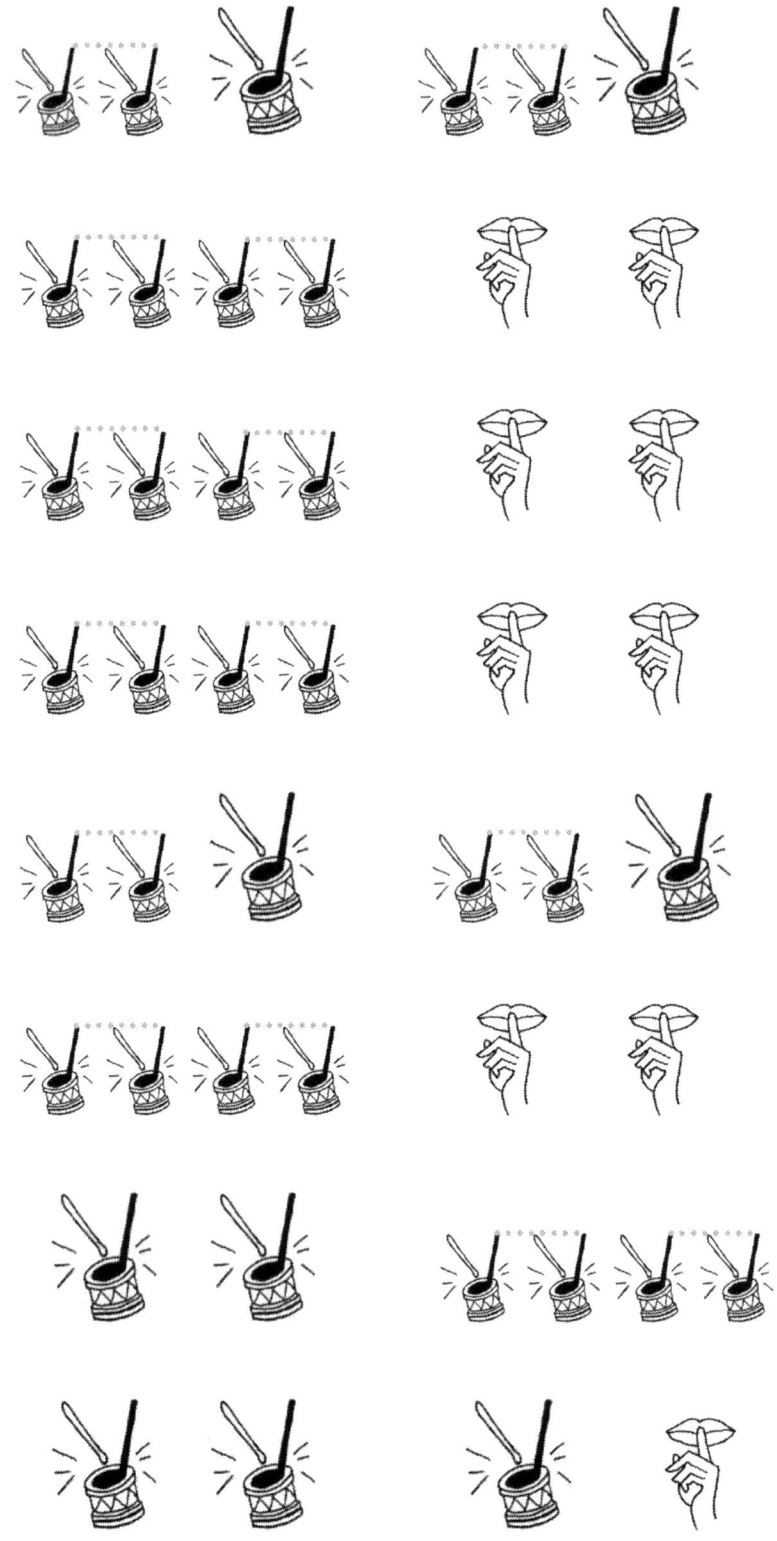

Body Scale: Jump Down to So

Last time we practiced stepping from "Do" down to "Ti" and back again. Did you know that you can jump even lower? Let's jump down from "Do" to low "So" by reaching down and touching our toes and then going back to "So" on our knees. Great job! Let's try starting on different "Do"s.

Color the "Do" boy red, the "So" boy blue!

Try these fun copycat phrases! **(See p. 43 for more copycat phrase)**

𝄞 Do   Do (Shh) Do   Do
       So   So

𝄞 Do   Do   Do   Re Mi
       So   So

𝄞 Do Re Mi Re Do   Do
                    So

𝄞   So Fa Mi Re Do   Do
                          So

Copyright 2015 Gregory Blankenbehler. All Rights Reserved. Photocopying Prohibited.

Frère Jacques / Are You Sleeping?

Suggested Order of Activities

1. Learn "bells" phrase "Ding, dong, ding!" with solfege and words and repeat as an ostinato.
2. Sight-read pictorial melody in solfege.
3. Sing melody with (English) words.
4. Perform with small group singing "bells" ostinato and the rest of the group singing melody.
5. Learn French words:

   Frère Jacques, frère Jacques,
       (frehr-uh zhah*-kuh)   * "zh" is the sound the "s" makes in the word "measure"
   Dormez-vous ? Dormez-vous ?
       (door-may voo)
   Sonnez les matines! Sonnez les matines!
       (soh*-nay lay muh-teen-uh)   *nasal "ohn" sound
   Ding, daing, dong. Ding, daing, dong.
       (ding*, dang, dong)   *go straight to the "ng" sound on each word and hold it to get the bell effect

6. Learn "bells" ostinato on piano with left hand (p. 35)
7. Learn the rest of melody on piano (p. 35)

Frère Jacques/Are You Sleeping?

Brother John is lots of fun to play with, but he doesn't like to get up in the morning. We need to ring the bells to wake him up!

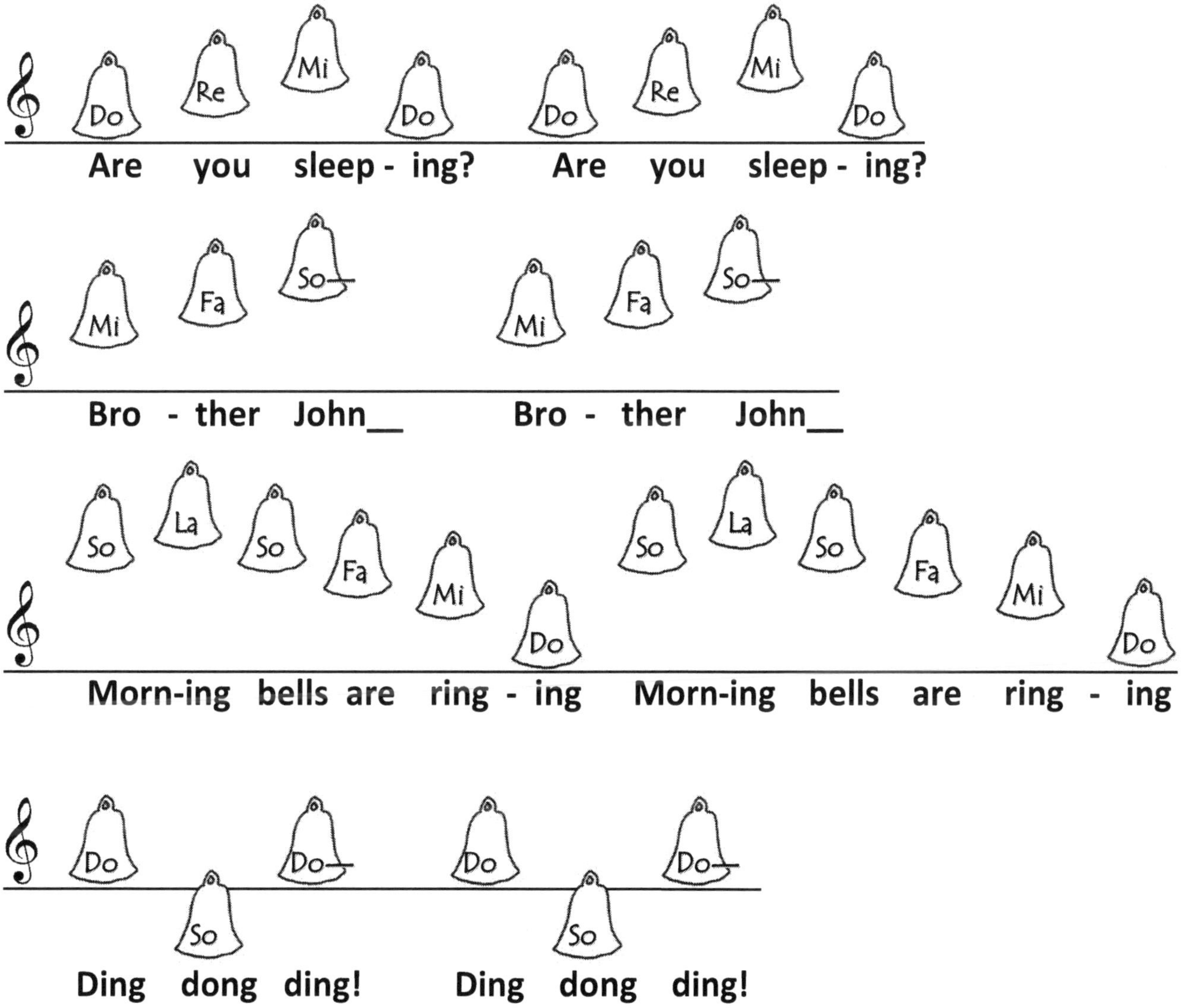

Do Re Mi Do | Do Re Mi Do
Are you sleep-ing? Are you sleep-ing?

Mi Fa So— | Mi Fa So—
Bro-ther John__ Bro-ther John__

So La So Fa Mi Do | So La So Fa Mi Do
Morn-ing bells are ring-ing Morn-ing bells are ring-ing

Do So Do | Do So Do
Ding dong ding! Ding dong ding!

Copyright 2015 Gregory Blankenbehler. All Rights Reserved. Photocopying Prohibited.

Frère Jacques – Piano

It's time to learn how to play a song on the piano! Curl your fingers like you are holding a big ball and tap each finger on the right key like a drum. It may be tricky at first to get your fingers to do what they're supposed to do, but keep practicing the song, repeating short phrases over and over again, until you do it without any mistakes.

Right thumb on Do (C) Find two black keys and tap on the white key to the left with your right thumb

Do/R1   Re/R2   Mi/R3   Do/R1   (Repeat)

Move thumb to Mi (E)

Mi/R1   Fa/R2   So/R3   (Repeat)

Left thumb on Do (C), Right fingers same position

So/R3   Fa/R2   Mi/R1   Do/L1   (Repeat)

Left fingers same position

Do/L1   So/L5   Do/L1

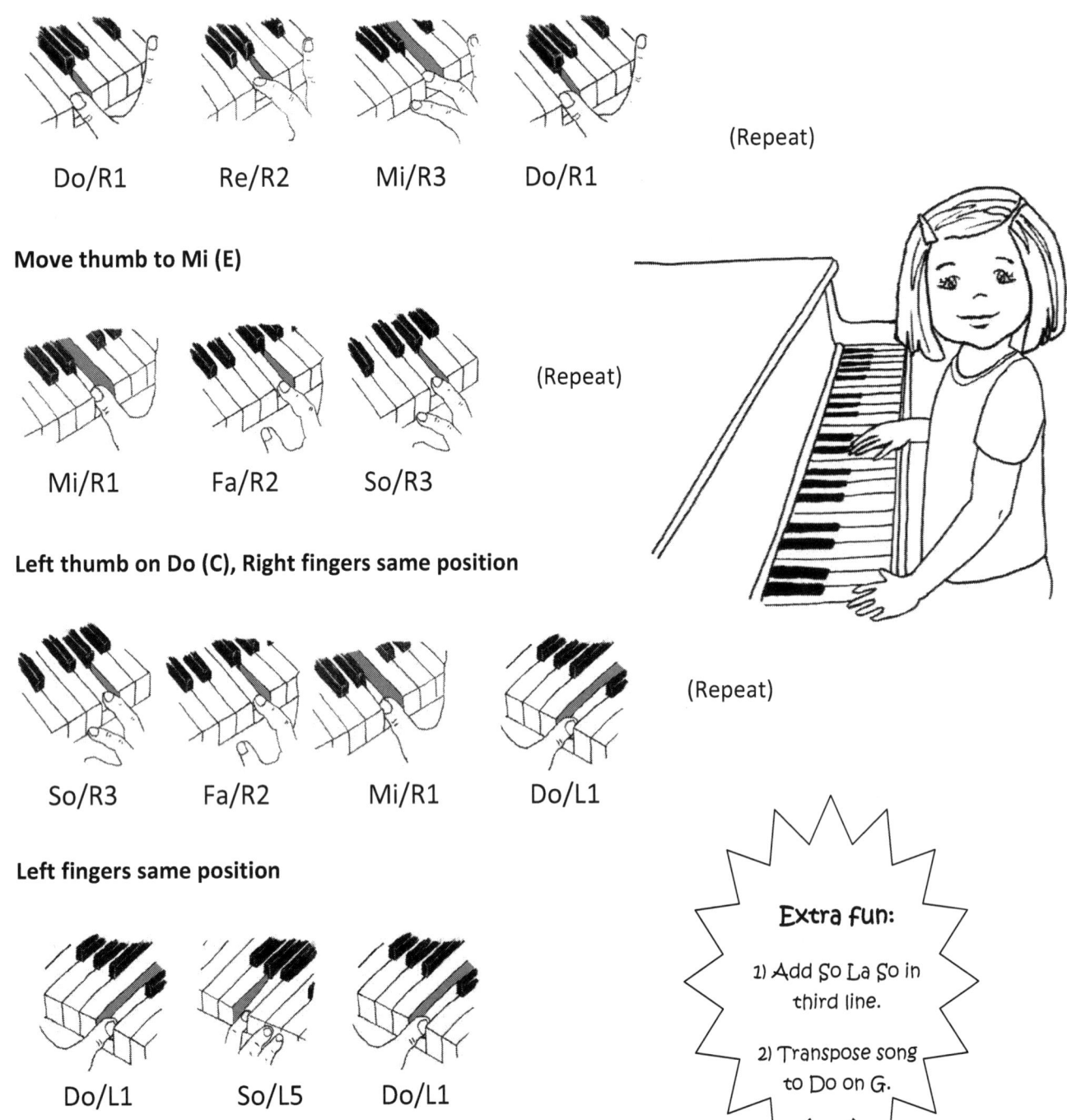

Extra fun:

1) Add So La So in third line.

2) Transpose song to Do on G.

Copyright 2015 Gregory Blankenbehler. All Rights Reserved. Photocopying Prohibited.

Gallop Game

Now we're going to play a game called "Gallop." But first, can you do the rhythm with your hands and knees? (right-left, right-left, right-left, shh)

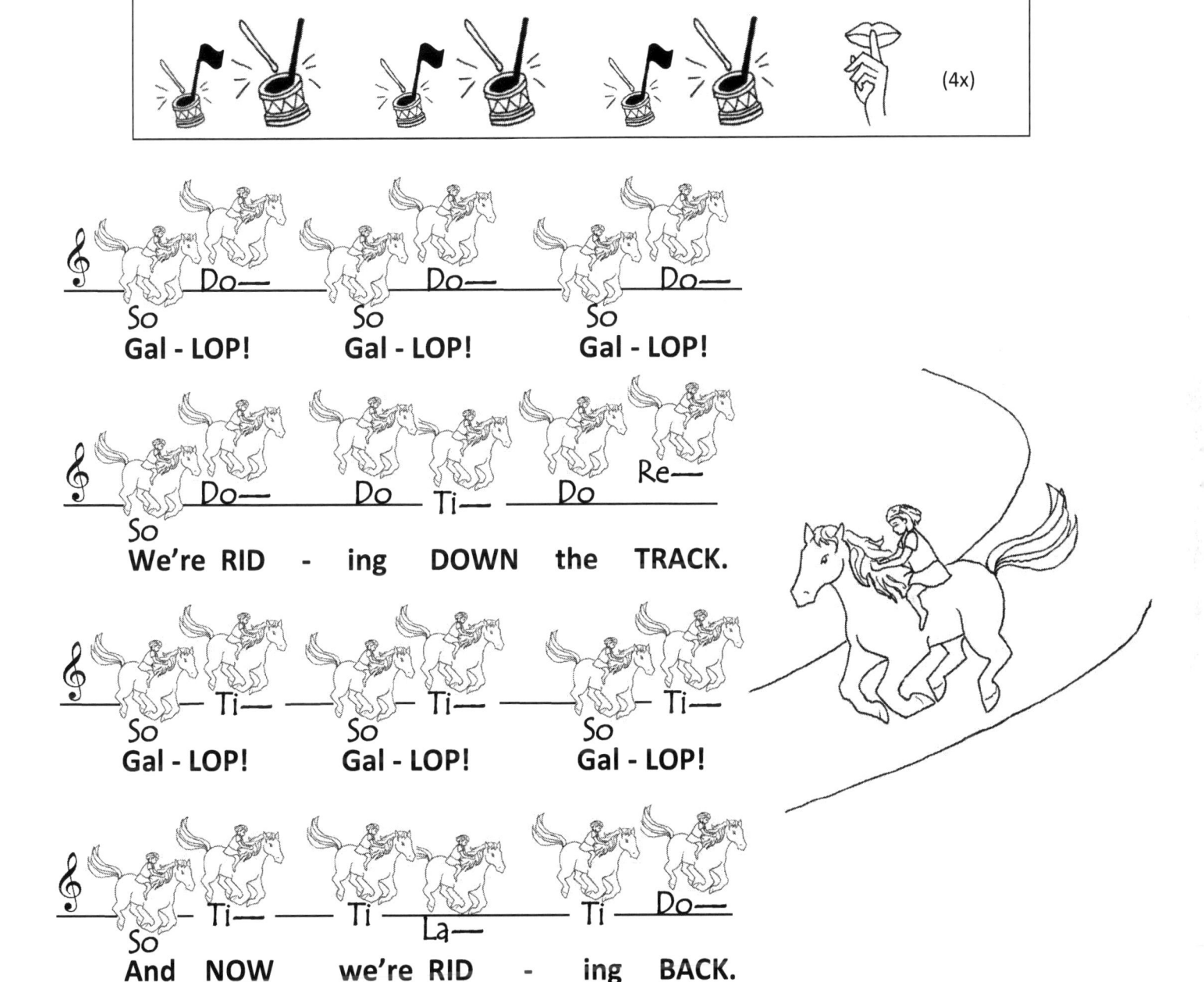

(4x)

| So | Do— | So | Do— | So | Do— |
| Gal - LOP! | Gal - LOP! | Gal - LOP! |

So | Do— | Do | Ti— | Do | Re—
We're RID - ing DOWN the TRACK.

So | Ti— | So | Ti— | So | Ti—
Gal - LOP! | Gal - LOP! | Gal - LOP!

So | Ti— | Ti La— | Ti | Do—
And NOW we're RID - ing BACK.

Teacher's Note:
To the tune of "La Raspa" (aka. "The Mexican Hat Dance") See p 37 for piano part and suggested order of activities.

"Gallop" Game: Class sits in two facing lines about 5 ft apart. As everyone sings and slaps, one student gallops up and back the "track" between the lines. As the student returns to their spot, the next student gets up and does the same on the next verse. Repeat until each student has a turn to be the "rider".

Copyright 2015 Gregory Blankenbehler. All Rights Reserved. Photocopying Prohibited.

Gallop!

Suggested Order of Activities

1. Sight read rhythm. ("Ti-Tah, Ti-Tah, Ti-tah, shh")
2. Slap rhythm with hands on knees. (right-left, right-left, right-left)
3. Sight read pictorial melody.
4. Sing song with words and slaps.
5. Play game (see p 36)

A-Hunting We Will Go

Suggested Order of Activities

1. Chant words with knee slaps (from "Gallop")
2. Sight-read pictorial melody
3. Sing song with words and slaps. (Sing the variant taught here! See p. 15.)
4. Play game:

   > Class stands in a circle and joins hands. One student is the "fox" who stands in the middle.
   > *"A-hunting we will go"* – everyone circles to the left
   > *"A-hunting we will go"* – everyone circles to the left
   > *"We'll catch a fox…"* – everyone steps towards the center of the circle
   > *"And then we'll let him go."* – everyone steps back out
   > During the next 8 beats the "fox" chooses a student and takes their place. That student goes to the center of the circle and is the new "fox." The song repeats until everyone has a turn as the "fox"

5. Make up new verses by inserting new animals and a place that rhymes.

A-Hunting We Will Go

Now we're going to learn another fun song with a game. We're going to go hunting and catch lots of animals. But don't worry, we'll always take care of them and let them go.

So / Do- / Do Do- / Do Do----
A - hunt - ing we will go!__

Re / Mi- / Mi Mi- / Mi Mi----
A - hunt - ing we will go!__

Fa / So- / So So- / So So So So So-
We'll catch a fox put him in a box

Fa Mi- / Mi Re- / Re Do----
And then we'll let him go!__

Make up a new verse!
We'll catch a **cat** and put him on a **mat**…
We'll catch a **frog** and put him on a **log**…

Copyright 2015 Gregory Blankenbehler. All Rights Reserved. Photocopying Prohibited.

Level C Readiness Assessment

Level B of *Singing Lessons for Little Singers* is designed to build upon the fundamentals of musicianship, vocal technique and performance introduced in Level A, preparing them to read music and sing songs of wider range and greater complexity. To be ready to begin Level C, students should be able to do each of the following:

	Ear Training
	Student can accurately repeat back "Copy Cat" melodic sequences (p. 43) with and without the Body Scale in multiple keys, high and low.
	Student can sing melody, harmony, and descant parts with solfege and lyrics together with others.
	Student can sing Level B songs and exercises with accurate pitches in multiple keys, high and low.
	Rhythm
	Student can accurately repeat back "Copy Cat" rhythmic sequences (p. 43) with rhythmic syllables, clapping, and simple percussion instruments (sticks, drums, etc.)
	Student can sing /play all Level B songs and exercises with accurate beat and rhythms.
	Sight-reading/Singing
	Student can accurately sight-sing all pictorially-notated songs and exercises in Level B.
	Student can accurately "sight-play" (on percussion instruments) and chant rhythmic syllables for all pictorially-notated songs and rhythm exercises, including all four sets of rhythm cards (p. 46).
	Technique
	Student demonstrates correct application of singing posture, "belly breathing," use of high and low voice, sustained support, and diction.
	Student can sing comfortably in both high and low voice, from B below middle C to E an octave and a 4th above.
	Student demonstrates correct use of simple percussion techniques in Level B songs and activities. (p. 22)
	Student can play "Frère Jacques" on piano using correct fingering. (p. 35)
	Performance
	Student can sing and perform all themed actions in Level B songs and activities.
	Student has performed several solos both in class and for family/friends at home.

If a student has a deficiency in any of these areas, it is recommended that the teacher take a few more lessons to focus on the skill in question before advancing the student on to Level C.

My Performance Record

Keep track of your performances by writing them down in the list below.

Date	Songs/Activities Performed	Audience

Certificate of Achievement in Music

Awarded to

_____

In recognition of their completion of

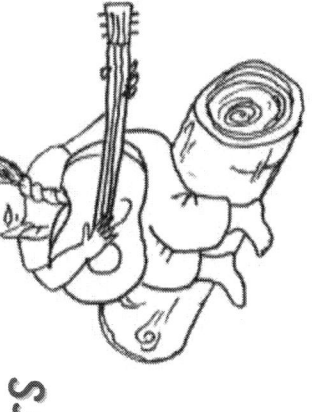

Singing Lessons for Little Singers

Level B

_____ _____
Teacher   Date

Singing Lessons for Little Singers

Very Young Beginner Series: Level B

Teacher Resources

"Copy Cat" Melodic and Rhythmic Sequences

Rhythm Cards

Lesson Plans

More Free Teacher Resources Available at www.LittleSingers.Info/Teachers

"Copy Cat" Melodic and Rhythmic Sequences

First introduced in Level A (p 18), "Copy Cat" is a crucial tool for ear and rhythm training. Sort of like "Simon Says," the teacher sings a short melodic or rhythmic sequence which the students then repeat back.

Example:

Teacher: "Now we're going to play Copy Cat. *Listen:* (sung) 'Mi-Fa-So-Fa-Mi-Fa-So.' *Sing*."

Student(s): "Mi-Fa-So-Fa-Mi-Fa-So."

T: "*Listen:* (sung) 'So-Mi-So-La-So-So-Do.' *Sing:*"

S: "So-Mi-So-La-So-So-Do"

T: "Good. *Listen:* (chanted) 'Ti-Ti Ti-Ti Tah Tah..' *Sing:*"

S: "Ti-Ti Ti-Ti Tah Tah." etc...

It is important that the teacher use the cues "*Listen*" and "*Sing*" so the students know when to listen and when to sing. Melodic sequences should typically be done with their accompanying Body Scale gesture in a comfortable, steady beat. Rhythmic sequences should be chanted (not sung to pitches) at a comfortable tempo.

Sequences to Prepare for "Sameer the Singer" and "I've Got Rhythms"

Melodic (Do-Mi-Fa-So-La):

Do Do Mi Mi So So Mi

So Mi Do Mi So Mi Do

So Mi So Mi Do Mi So

Mi Mi So So Do Do Do

Do Mi So La So Mi Do

So La So Mi Do Mi Do

So Fa Mi Fa So La So

So So Fa Fa Mi Mi Do

Mi Fa So La So So Do

Do Do So So La So Fa

Do Do So Mi Fa Fa Mi

La So Fa Mi Fa So La

Transpose sequences for different "Copy Cat" sessions to work high and low voice.
Feel free to create new sequences using the same solfege syllables.

Teacher Resources — 44

Rhythms (review):

4/4 ♩ ♩ ♩ ♩ | ♩ ♩ ♩ 𝄽 ‖ Tah Tah Tah Tah Tah_ah Tah (shh)	4/4 ♩ ♩ | ♫ ♫ ♩ 𝄽 ‖ Tah_ah Tah_ah Ti-Ti Ti-Ti Tah (shh)	4/4 ♫ ♫ ♩ ♩ | ♩ 𝄽 𝄽 𝄽 ‖ Ti-Ti Ti-Ti Tah (shh) Tah (shh) (shh) (shh)
4/4 ♩ ♩ ♩ | ♩ 𝄽 ♩ 𝄽 ‖ Tah_ah Tah (shh) Tah (shh) Tah (shh)	4/4 ♩ ♩ ♩ | 𝄽 ♫ ♩ 𝄽 ‖ Tah Tah Tah_ah (shh) Ti-Ti Tah (shh)	4/4 ♩ ♩ ♫ ♫ | ♫ ♩ ♩ 𝄽 ‖ Tah Tah Ti-ti Ti-Ti Ti-Ti Tah Tah (shh)
4/4 ♩ ♫ ♫ ♩ | ♩ ♩ 𝄽 𝄽 ‖ Tah Ti-ti Ti-Ti Tah Tah Tah (shh) (shh)	4/4 𝄽 𝄽 ♩ | ♩ ♩ ♩ ‖ Tah_ah Tah Tah Tah (shh)	4/4 ♩ ♩ ♩ ♫ | ♩ ♫ ♩ 𝄽 ‖ Tah Tah Ti Ti-Ti -Tah Ti-Ti Tah (shh)

Sequences to Prepare for "Grand Old Duke of York" and "Kumbaya," and "Twinkle, Twinkle Little Star"

Melodic (Do-Re-Mi-Fa-So-La):

Do Re Mi Re Do Do Do	Do Re Mi Fa So La So	Mi Re Do Re Mi Fa So
So La So Fa Mi Re Do	So Mi Do Re Mi Re Do	Mi Re Mi Fa Re Re Do
Do Re Do Re Mi Fa Mi	Fa Fa Mi Mi Re Re Do	So Fa Mi Do Re Re Mi
Do Do Re Re Mi Mi Fa	So La So Mi Re Do Do	Do Re Mi So La Fa So

Rhythms:

4/4 ♩ ♩ ♫ ♩ | ♫ ♫ ♫ 𝄽 ‖ Tah Tah Ti-Ti Tah Ti-Ti Ti-Ti Ti-Ti (shh)	4/4 ♫ ♫ ♫ ♫ | 𝄽 ♩ ♫ 𝄽 ‖ Ti-Ti Ti-Ti (shh) Tah_ah Ti-Ti (shh)	4/4 ♫ ♩ ♩ ♫ | ♩ 𝄽 𝄽 ‖ Ti-Ti Tah Tah Ti-Ti Tah_ah (shh) (shh)
4/4 ♫ ♩ ♫ ♩ | 𝄽 ♩ ♩ 𝄽 ‖ Ti-Ti Tah Ti-Ti Tah (shh) Tah Tah (shh)	4/4 ♩ ♫ ♩ ♫ | ♩ ♫ ♩ 𝄽 ‖ Tah Ti-Ti Tah Ti-Ti Tah Ti-Ti Tah (shh)	4/4 ♫ ♩ ♩ ♩ | ♫ ♩ ♩ 𝄽 ‖ Ti-Ti Tah Tah Tah Ti-Ti Tah Tah (shh)
4/4 ♫ ♩ ♫ ♩ | ♫ ♩ 𝄽 𝄽 ‖ Ti-Ti Tah Ti-Ti Tah Ti Ti Tah (shh) (shh)	4/4 𝄽 ♫ 𝄽 | ♫ ♫ ♩ ‖ (shh) Ti-Ti Ti-Ti (shh) Ti Ti Ti-Ti Tah_ah	4/4 ♩ ♫ ♩ 𝄽 | 𝄽 ♫ ♩ ‖ Tah Ti-Ti Tah (shh) (shh) Ti-Ti Tah_ah

Sequences to Prepare for "Go to the Circus," "Frère Jacques," and "A-Hunting We Will Go

Melodic (↓So-↓Ti-Do-Re-Mi-Fa-So-La):

Do Ti Do Re Mi Fa So

Mi Re Do Ti Do Do Do

Do Ti Do Mi Re Mi Do

La So Mi Do Re Ti Do

Fa Mi Re Do Ti Ti Do

Re Do Ti Re Do Re Mi

Do So Do Re Mi Fa So

Mi Mi Re Re Do So Do

Do So Do So Do Re Mi

Re Do So Do Re Mi Do

Do Ti Do So Do Re Mi

So La So Mi Do So Do

Rhythms:

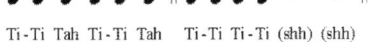

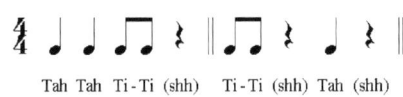

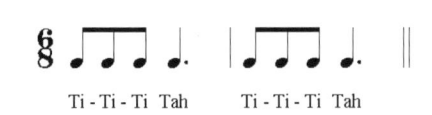

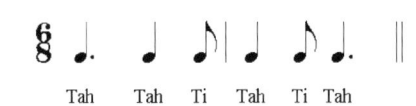

Ti-Ti Tah Ti-Ti Tah Ti-Ti Ti-Ti (shh) (shh)

Tah Tah Ti-Ti (shh) Ti-Ti (shh) Tah (shh)

Ti-Ti Ti-Ti Tah (shh) Tah Ti-Ti (shh) (shh)

Ti-Ti-Ti Ti-Ti-Ti Tah Tah

Ti-Ti-Ti Tah Ti-Ti-Ti Tah

Ti-Ti-Ti Tah Tah Tah

Tah Ti Tah Ti Tah Tah

Tah Tah Ti Tah Ti Tah

Tah Tah Ti Tah (shh)

Teacher Resources — 46

Rhythm Cards

Introduced on p. 10, Rhythm Cards are a very effective tool for acquiring and improving fluid rhythm reading. They are provided on the next 8 pages to be photocopied (enlarged, if wished), and cut out along the dotted lines.

While rhythm cards can be used in "flashcard" mode to practice identifying individual rhythms, they are most effective when strung together to create unique rhythmic combinations.

For example, the teacher may draw four rhythm cards at random out of a stack including set 1 and 2 cards. Placing them next to each other, they might look like this:

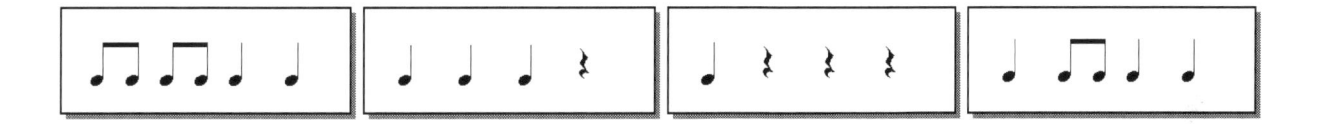

Together or individually, the students can either point and say or look and play the resulting four-measure rhythm:

Ti-Ti Ti-Ti Tah Tah | Tah Tah Tah (shh) | Tah (shh) (shh) (shh) | Tah Ti-Ti Tah Tah

Tips for success:

- Start practicing with one and then two-card combinations before attempting four cards.
- Always keep the beat study when passing from one card to the next, just as if they were measures of a song.
- Use the rhythm syllables taught in Little Singers (quarter=Tah, eighth=Ti, half=Tah-ah, quarter rest=shh or silence)
- Move along in units of a beat. In other words, look at eighth notes pairs as one object that goes "Ti-Ti."

Set 1

Singing Lessons for Little Singers™ – Level B

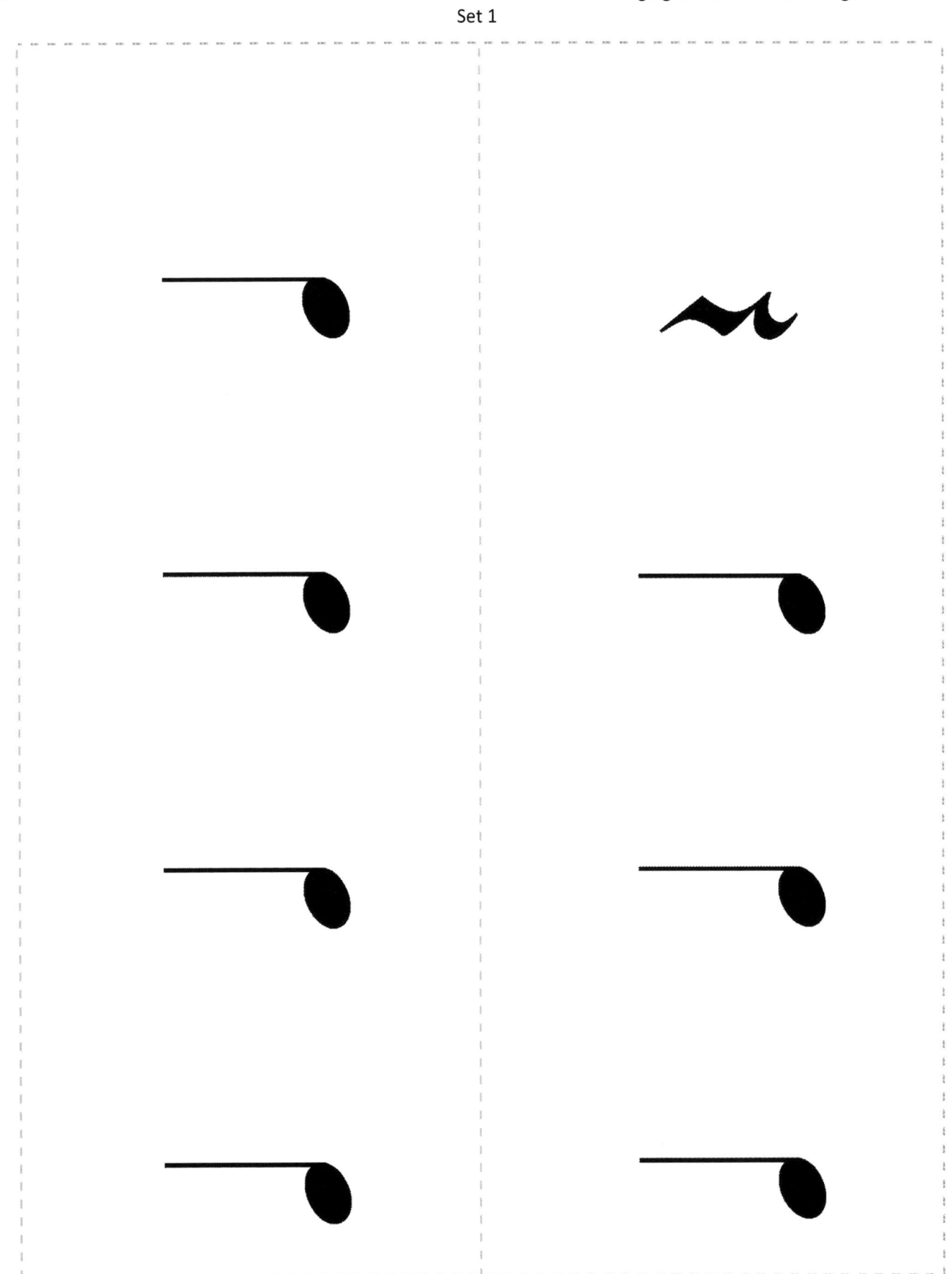

Copyright 2014 Gregory Blankenbehler. Permission granted to photocopy this page for use in singing lessons.

Rhythm Cards

Set 1

Teacher Resources – 48

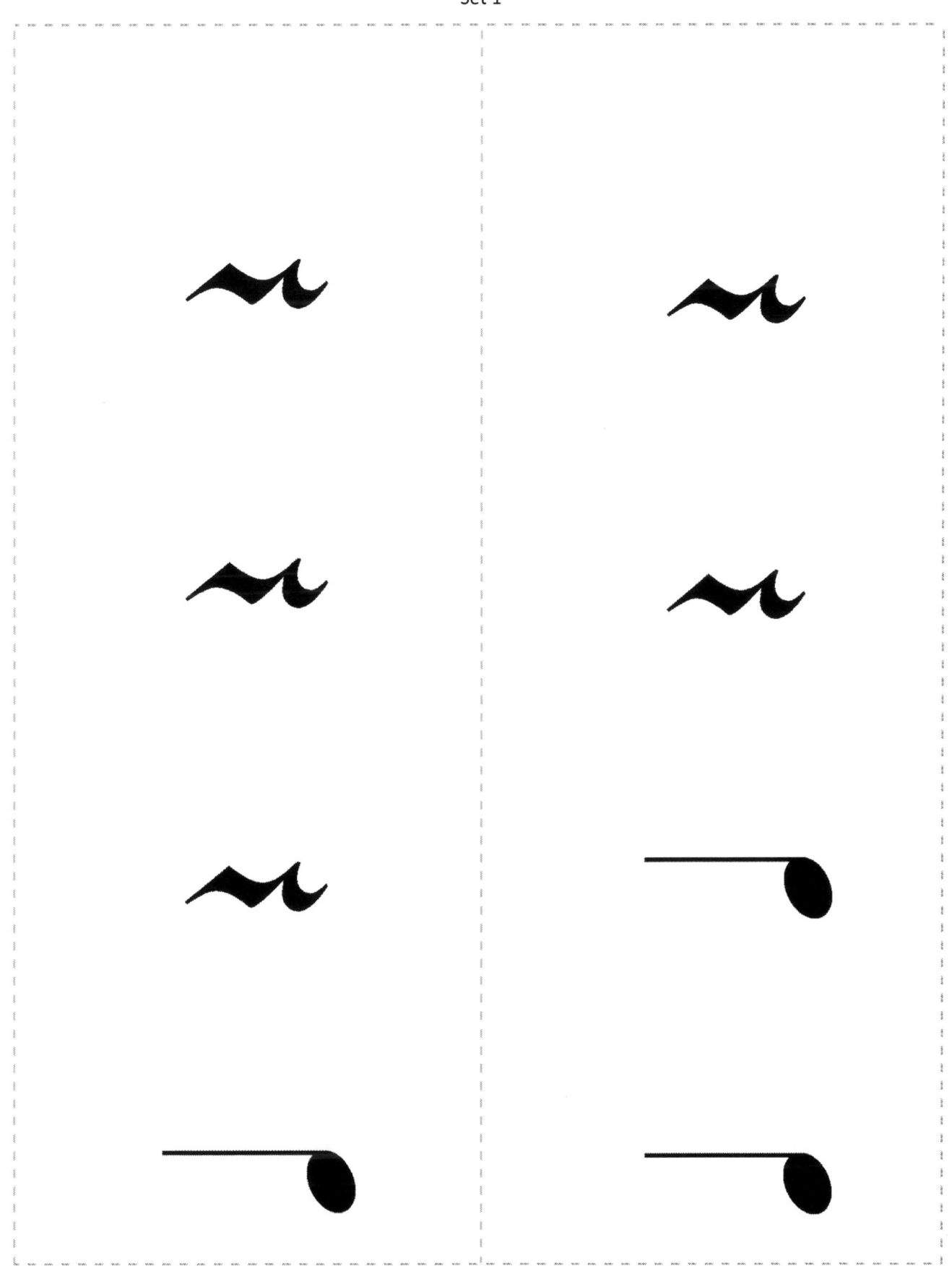

Copyright 2014 Gregory Blankenbehler. Permission granted to photocopy for use in singing lessons.

Set 2

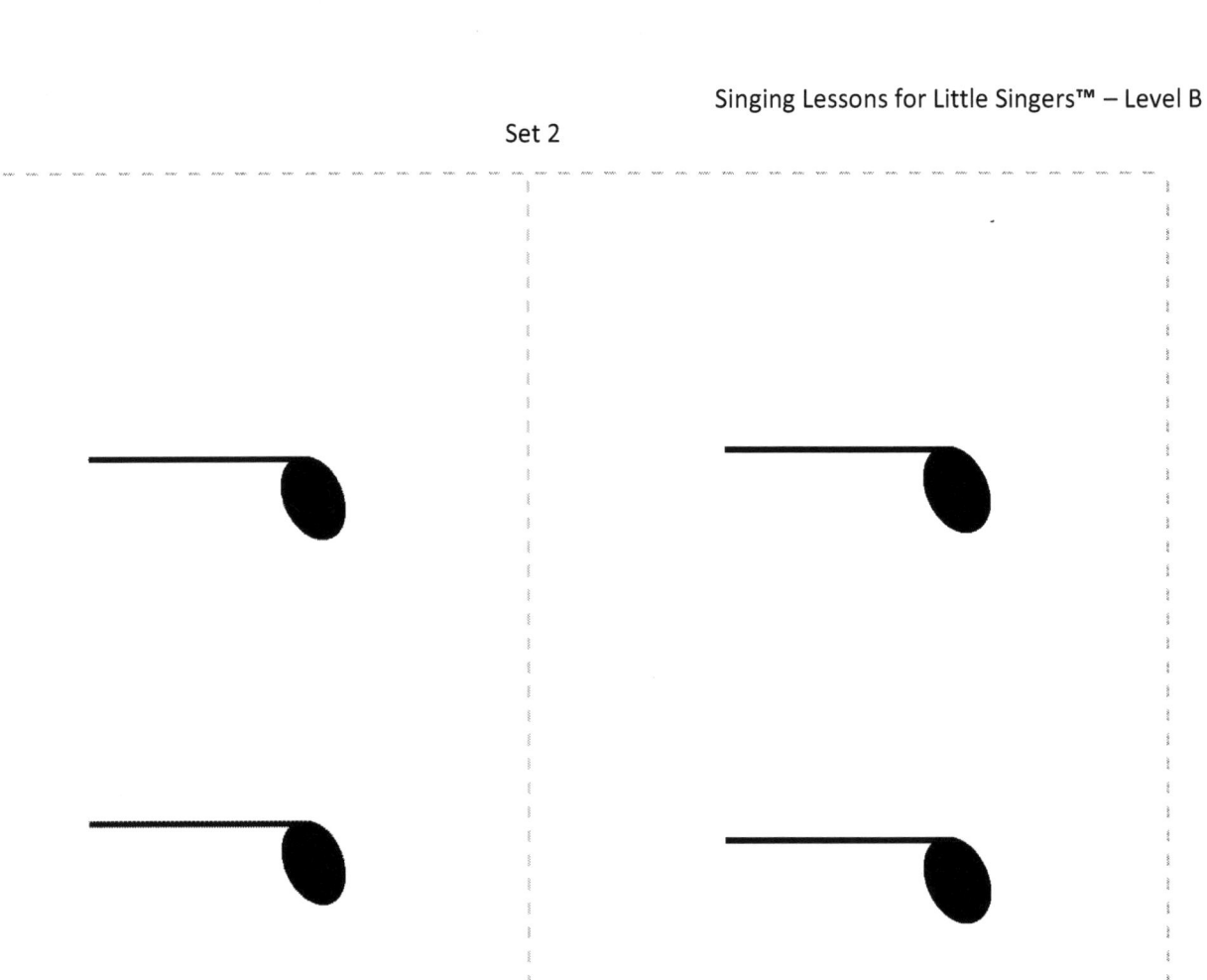

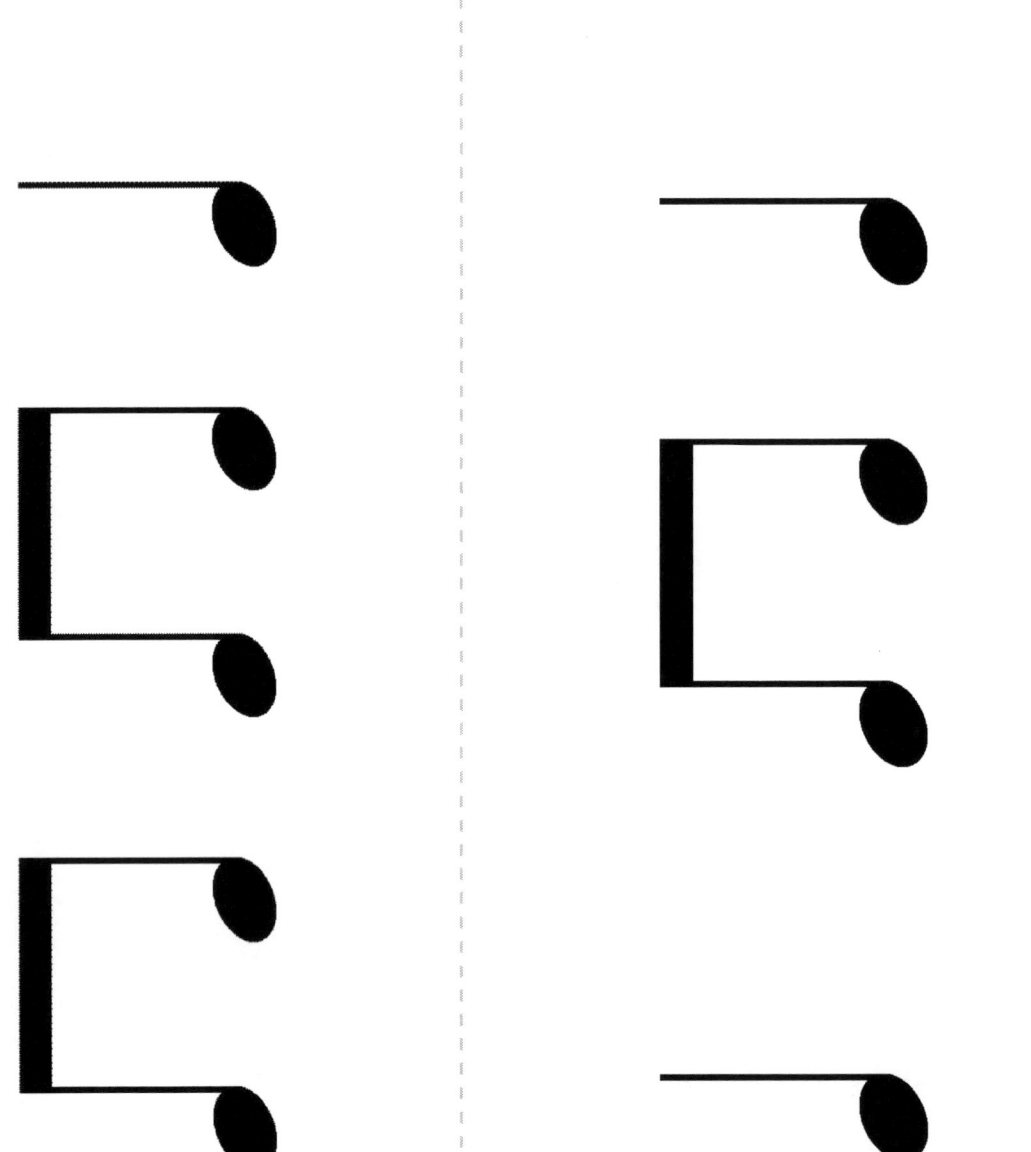

Rhythm Cards

Teacher Resources – 50

Set 2

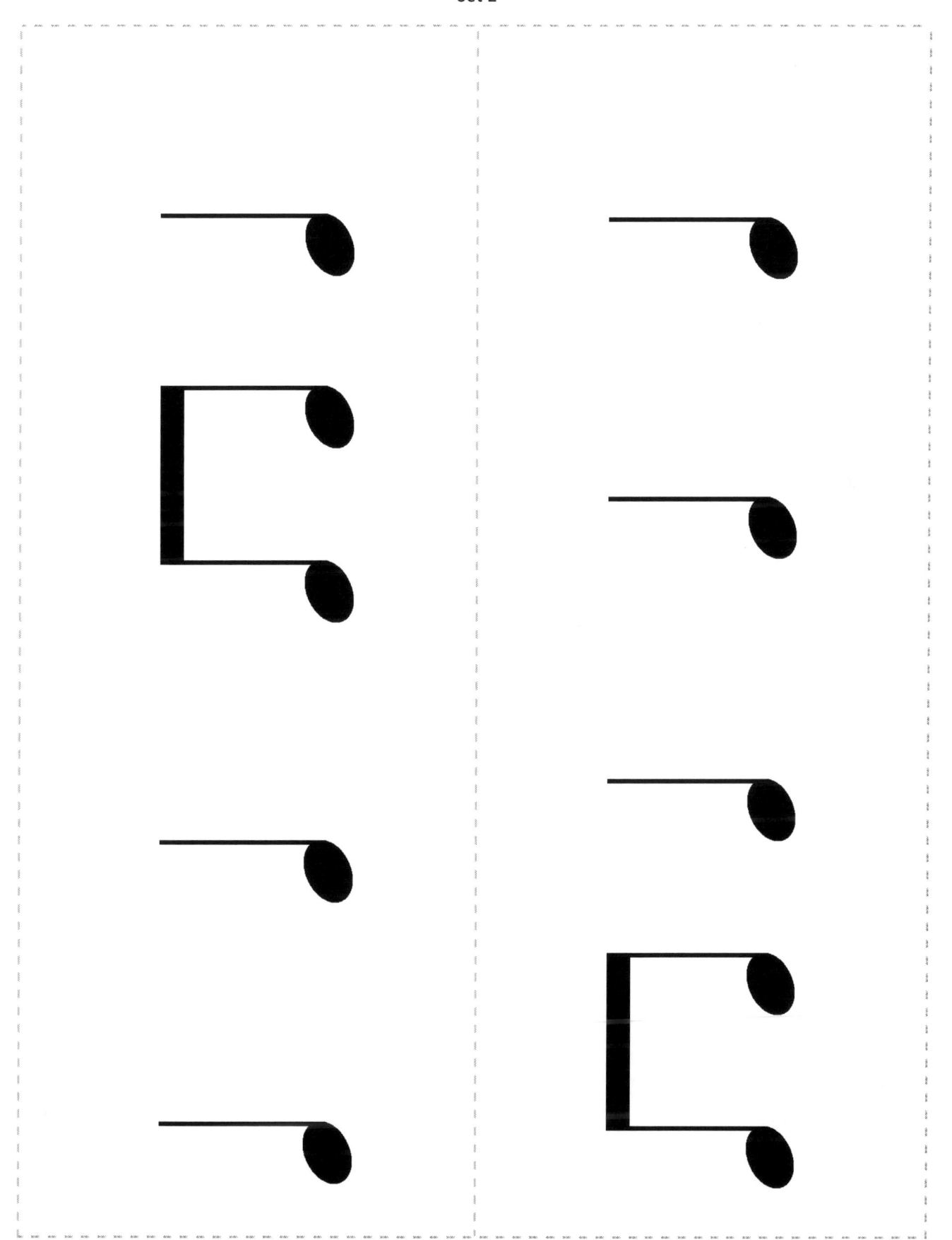

Copyright 2014 Gregory Blankenbehler. Permission granted to photocopy for use in singing lessons.

Set 3

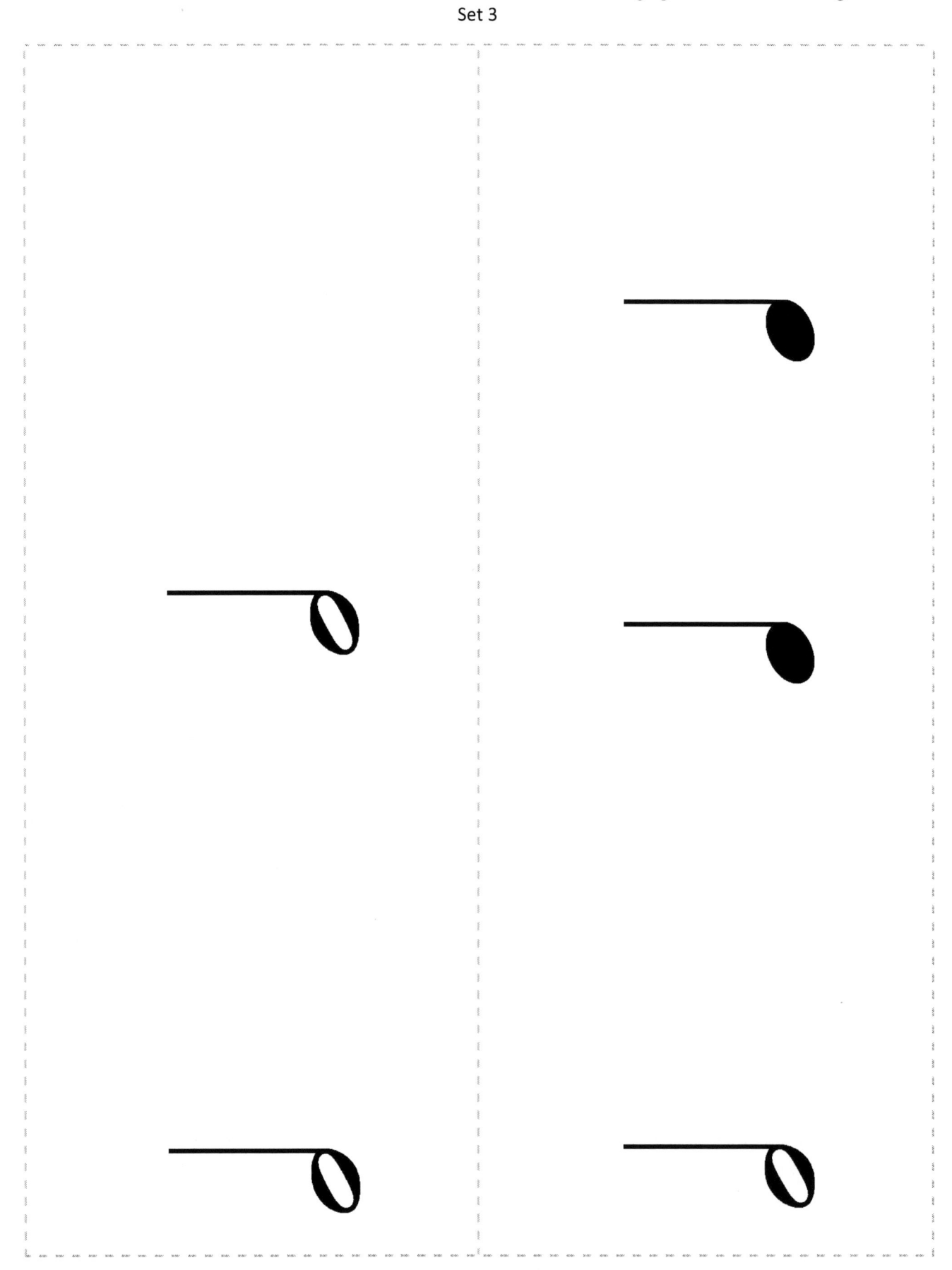

Rhythm Cards

Teacher Resources – 52

Set 3

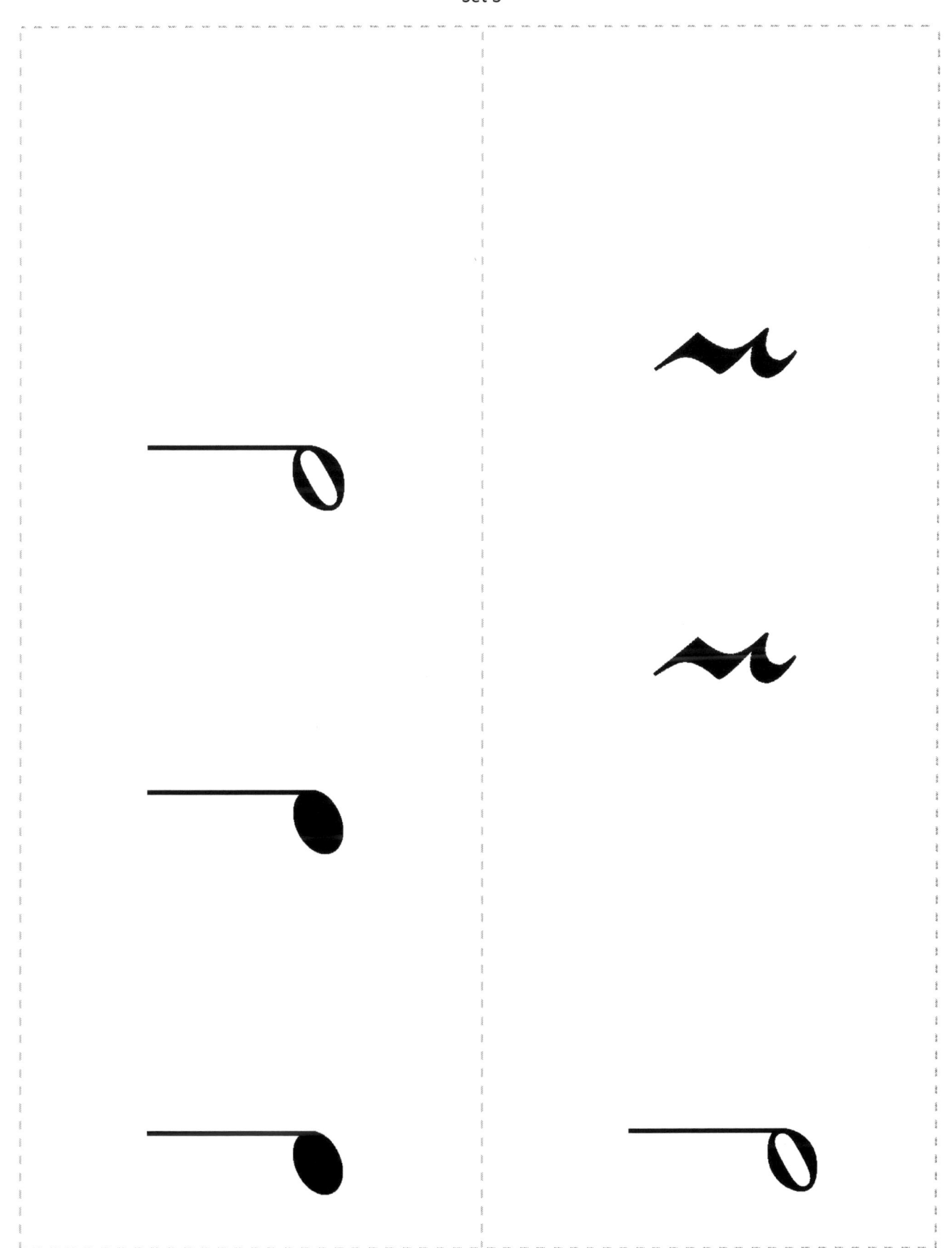

Copyright 2014 Gregory Blankenbehler. Permission granted to photocopy for use in singing lessons.

Set 4

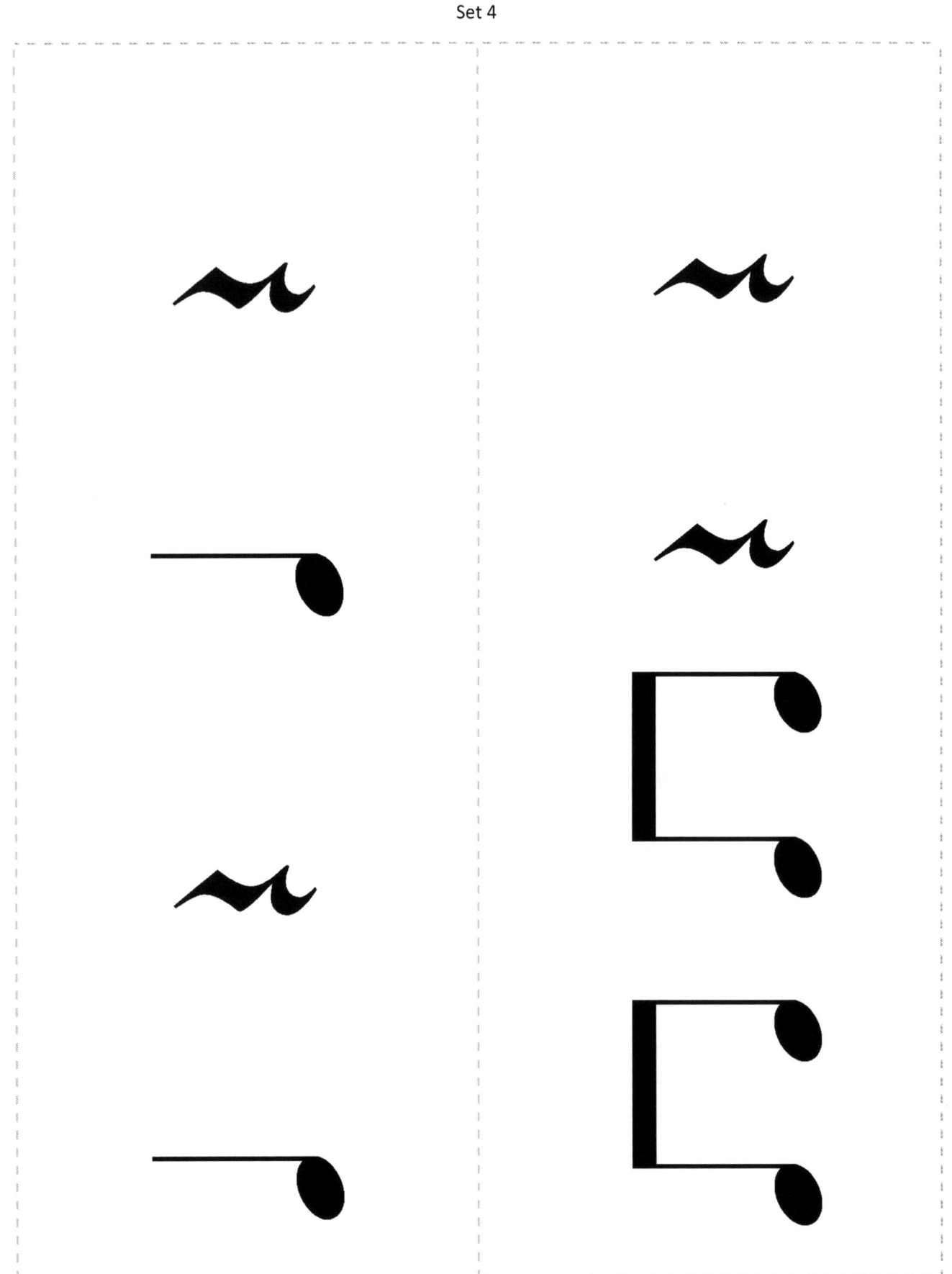

Singing Lessons for Little Singers™ – Level B

Copyright 2014 Gregory Blankenbehler. Permission granted to photocopy this page for use in singing lessons.

Rhythm Cards

Teacher Resources – 54

Set 4

Copyright 2014 Gregory Blankenbehler. Permission granted to photocopy for use in singing lessons.

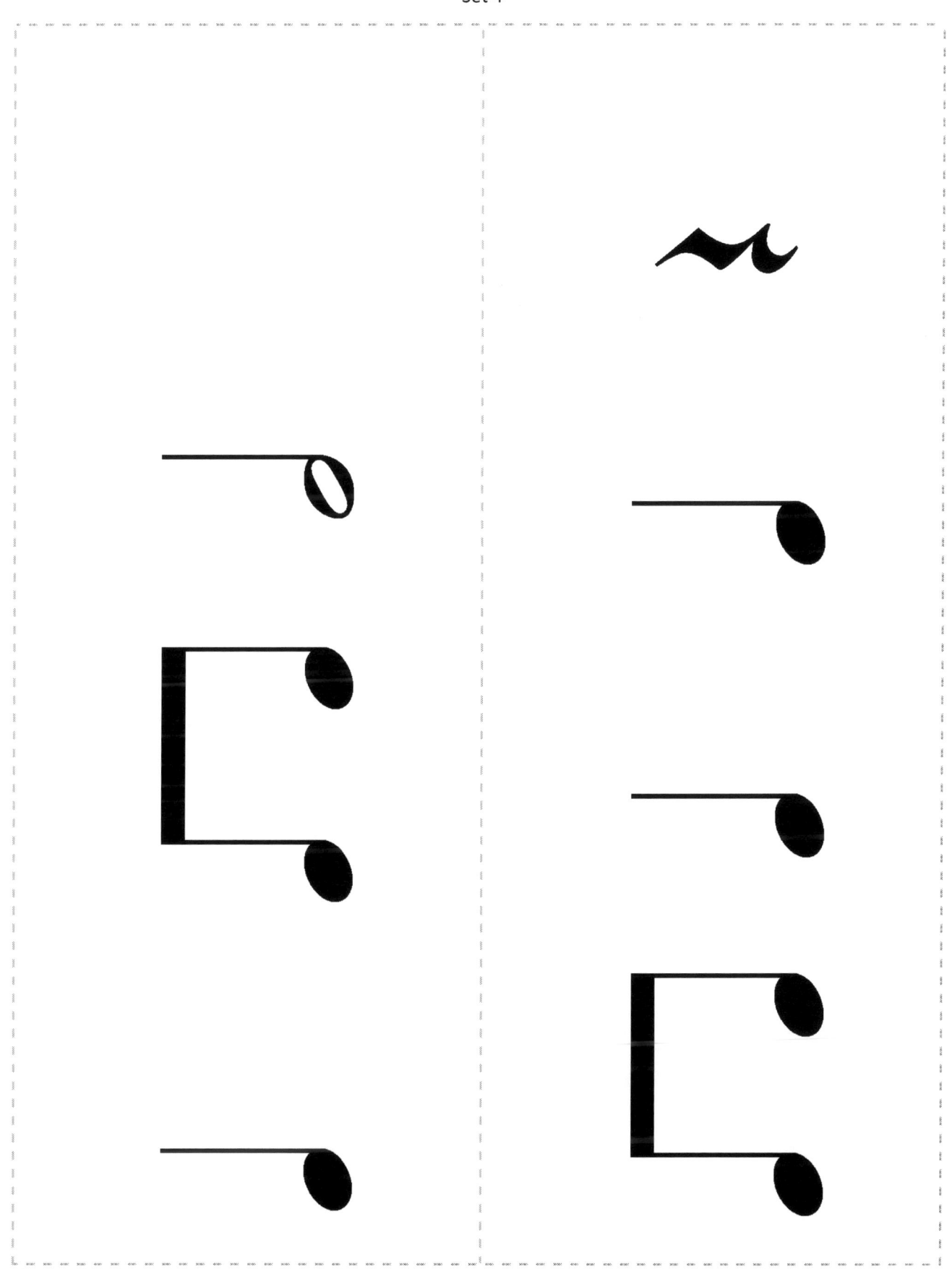

Lesson Plans

As in Level A, these lessons plans have been created as a guide to help teachers pace and balance their lessons with the skills being taught. It is especially important that teachers pay close attention to unit and lesson objectives to ensure that their lessons are focused on developing the correct skills. The pace of these lessons has been set purposefully slow to accommodate slower learners; teachers should feel free to accelerate them as needed.

===

Unit 1:

- PERFORMANCE: Review lesson routines and expectations: following directions, taking turns, practicing, performing, etc.
- TECHNIQUE: Review basic singing techniques of posture, belly breathing, and sustained tones.
- TECHNIQUE: Review singing in high and low voices.
- EAR TRAINING: Review known Body Scale (D-M-F-S-L) and derivative melodic sequences in various keys.
- RHYTHM: Review basic rhythm syllables and repeat back copycat rhythms.
- SIGHT-READING: Read basic rhythmic notation on p. 10 and rhythm cards (see p 10).
- PERFORMANCE: Learn and perform individual and group parts in songs.

Lesson #1

Objectives: Students[1] will

- PER: Reorient to following singing lessons procedures and expectations in class and practicing at home.
- TECH: Review and correct singing posture through "windmills" and other singing activities.
- TECH: Review and correct breathing technique through "windmills" and "Sameer" activities.
- EAR: Review D-M-F-S-L body scale names, pitches, and gestures.
- EAR: Repeat back text as spoken by teacher.
- TECH: Review singing in high voice on body scale and "Sameer."
- PER: Begin learning "Sameer…" and participate in performing "Ring Around the Rosie."

Parents will:

- Recommit to do assigned activities in short practice-play sessions at home during the next week.

Activities:

1. Welcome students and parents back for Level B. Redo introductions for any new students.
2. Remind parents the importance of their attention in class and their leadership in facilitating their child's practice-play sessions at home. Ask them to commit to a certain number of short practice-play sessions this next week.
3. Lead/Reteach students "Stretch and Stand Up Straight" activity from Level A (p 5). Review good posture. (Level B – p 5)
4. Review "belly breathing" technique using good posture and long hisses. (p 5)
5. Teach "windmills," (p 5) adding to the actions hissing and eventually pitched hums and "whoo"s when students are ready.
6. Read story of "Sameer the Singer." (p 8)
7. Chant V1 of "Sameer…" in call & response with even, sustained phrasing. (Make up actions if desired.)
8. Review names, pitches, and gestures for known Body Scale steps: D-M-F-S-L. Do=C (p 6)
9. Sing Body Scale in Do=F and G using high voice as needed. Review how to sing in high voice. (p 6)
10. Chant V2 of "Sameer…" in call & response.
11. Lead class in performing "Ring Around the Rosies" from Level A with advanced actions, changing keys, and solo roles if possible.
12. Give parents home assignments and remind of commitment to practice a certain number of days.

Assignments (for Parents to do with Child at Home):

- Practice posture and belly-breathing techniques while standing still and hissing/humming. (p 5)
- Practice "Windmills." (p 5)
- Read the story to "Sameer the Singer" (p 8) and practice chanting verses in call & response.
- Color in "Sameer…" picture (p 8) and p 5 pictures.

---

[1] While Level B can be effectively used for either group or solo private lessons, these lesson plans will refer to students and parents in the plural. Teachers of single students should make appropriate adaptations.

Lesson #2

Objectives: Students will

- PER: Continue to follow singing lessons routines and expectations.
- TECH: Review posture, belly-breathing, sustained phrases.
- EAR: Review Body Scale solfege and apply to "Sameer…"
- PER: Practice words and learn solfege for "Sameer…"
- PER: Take part in performing "Ring Around the Rosie" or another similar song.

Activities:

1. "Stretch and Stand Up Straight" followed by belly-breathing with sustained hissing and humming.
2. Review "Windmills" motions and add breathing and hissing/humming at correct times. (p 5)
3. Chant "Sameer the Singer" V1 in call & response.
4. Review Body Scale (p 6) in Do=C.
5. Teach "Sameer…" solfege (see p 8) using call & response by rote. (use body scale gestures)
6. Chant "Sameer…" V2 in call & response.
7. Sing Body Scale in Do=F and G.
8. Sing "Sameer…" V1 and V2 (words with pitches): V1 in Do=C, V2 in Do=F.
9. Perform "Ring Around the Rosie" or "My Robot" from Level A.
10. Give parents home assignments.

Assignments:

- Practice posture and belly-breathing techniques while standing still and hissing/humming. (p 5)
- Practice "Windmills" with hissing/humming. (p 5)
- Practice chanting words, singing solfege, and singing words for "Sameer…" V1 and V2.
- Color Body Scale steps for Do, Mi, Fa, So, and La in picture as indicated on p 6.

Lesson #3

Objectives: Students will

- TECH: Review and coordinate posture, belly-breathing, sustained phrases.
- PER: Practice words and solfege for "Sameer…"
- RHY: Review rhythmic syllables and durations.
- EAR/RHY: Practice copycat sequences for "Sameer/I've Got Rhythms."
- PER: Learn and perform words to "I've Got Rhythms."
- PER: Take part in performing "Ring Around the Rosie" or other similar song.

Activities:

1. "Stretch and Stand Up Straight" followed by belly-breathing with sustained hissing and humming.
2. "Windmills" coordinating motions with breathing and hissing/humming. (p 5)
3. "Sameer…" solfege.
4. "Sameer…" words and music V1 (Do=C) and V2 (Do=F).
5. Reintroduce "Copycat" activity. (p 9) Practice some of the melodic copycat sequences for "Sameer/I've Got Rhythms." (p 43)
6. Reintroduce rhythm syllables through copycat. Practice some of the rhythmic copycat sequences for "Sameer/I've Got Rhythms" on top of p 44.
7. Read story of "I've Got Rhythms." (p 12)
8. Learn words of "I've Got Rhythms" in rhythm through call & response.
9. Perform "Ring Around the Rosie" or other favorite song.

Assignments:

- Practice "Windmills" as done in class. (p 5)
- Sing "Sameer…" solfege and words, in correct keys if possible, in call & response.
- Color "copycat" picture. (p 9)

Lesson #4

Objectives: Students will

- TECH: Coordinate posture, belly-breathing, and sustained phrases.
- PER: Perform "Sameer…"
- EAR/RHY: Repeat back copycat sequences.
- SR: Teach basic rhythm reading.
- SR: Read rhythm card #1 and #2
- PER: Learn and perform words and solfege to "I've Got Rhythms."
- PER: Take part in performing "Ring Around the Rosie" or other similar song.

Activities:

1. "Stretch and Stand Up Straight" followed by belly-breathing with sustained hissing and humming.
2. "Windmills" coordinating motions with breathing and hissing/humming. (p 5)
3. "Sameer" V1 and V2.
4. Copycat sequences for "Sameer…" etc. (p 43-44)

Copyright 2015 Greg Blankenbehler, All Rights Reserved.

5. Teach/Review "Rhythm Reading," using point & say. (p 10)
6. Point & say rhythm cards #1 and #2 separate and together. (See p 46)
7. Read story to "I've Got Rhythms."
8. Chant words to "I've Got Rhythms" in rhythm.
9. Teach solfege using call & response by rote.
10. Perform "Ring Around the Rosie" or other favorite song.

Assignments:

- Practice "Windmills" coordinating motions with breathing and hissing/humming.
- Practice "Rhythm Reading" (p 10) and Rhythm Cards #1-2 in set 1.
- Practice words and solfege for "I've Got Rhythms."
- Color "Rhythm Cards" picture. (p 10)

Lesson #5

Objectives: Students will

- TECH: Coordinate posture, belly-breathing, and sustained phrases.
- EAR/RHY: Repeat back copycat sequences.
- SR: Point & say and look & clap reading "Rhythm Reading." (p 10)
- SR: Point & say set 1 rhythm cards alone and in combinations of two.
- PER: Perform solfege and words with pitches on "I've Got Rhythms."
- PER: Perform rhythm cards set 1 to "I've Got Rhythms."
- PER: Perform "Sameer" with some students taking the leader role.

Activities:

1. "Stretch and Stand Up Straight" followed by belly-breathing with sustained hissing and humming.
2. "Windmills" coordinating motions with breathing and hissing/humming. (p 5)
3. Copycat sequences for "Sameer..." (p 43-44)
4. Rhythm Reading" (p 10) using point & say and look & clap.
5. Rhythm cards set 1 (p 47-48) separately and in combinations of two.
6. Solfege for "I've Got Rhythms."
7. Words and pitches for "I've Got Rhythms" in call & response.

8. Do rhythm cards to accompaniment of "I've Got Rhythms," as explained in Activity #3. (p 11)
9. Perform "Sameer." Let students take turns singing first if they are ready.

Assignments:

- Practice "Windmills" coordinating motions with breathing and hissing/humming.
- Sing "I've Got Rhythms."
- Practice rhythm cards set 1.
- Color "I've Got Rhythms" picture. (p 12)

Lesson #6

Objectives: Students will

- TECH: Coordinate posture, belly-breathing, and sustained phrases.
- EAR/RHY: Repeat back new copycat sequences.
- SR: Point & say set 1 rhythm cards in combos of 2 and 4; point & say first two cards of set 2.
- PER: Perform "I've Got Rhythms" with words and set 1 rhythm cards.
- SR: Learn 8th note pairs on set 2 rhythm cards.

Activities:

1. "Stretch and Stand Up Straight" followed by belly-breathing with sustained hissing and humming.
2. "Windmills" coordinating motions with breathing and hissing/humming. (p 5)
3. Copycat melodic sequences for "Sameer." Begin practicing copycat rhythm sequences for "Grand Old Duke..." etc. (p 44)
4. Rhythm cards set 1 in combos of 2 and 4.
5. "I've Got Rhythms" words and set 1 rhythm cards.
6. Introduce first two rhythm cards of set 2. (p 49) Explain 8th note pairs.
7. Read story to "Grand Old Duke..." (p 16)
8. Perform "Sameer," letting students take turns as leader.

Assignments:

- Practice "Windmills" (p 5) Practice "Windmills" coordinating motions with breathing and hissing/humming.
- Practice rhythm cards set 1 and first 2 cards of set 2.
- Sing "Sameer."
- Sing "I've Got Rhythms."

Unit 2:

- TECHNIQUE: Refine basic singing techniques of posture, belly breathing, and sustained tones.
- EAR TRAINGING: Learn "Re" step of the Body Scale.
- EAR TRAINING: Become proficient at increasingly difficult melodic and rhythmic sequences.
- SIGHT READING: Read increasingly difficult rhythmic notation and pictorial solfege notation.
- PERFORMANCE: Learn and perform basic percussion technique.
- PERFORMANCE: Learn and perform simple descants and harmony parts sung by themselves.
- PERFORMANCE: Take unique parts in performances combining melody and descant/harmony singing, movement, and percussion parts.

Lesson #7

Objectives: Students will

- TECH: Coordinate posture, belly-breathing, and sustained phrases.
- EAR/RHY: Repeat back copycat sequences.
- SR: Point & say set 1 rhythm cards in combos of 4; point & say all set 2 cards.
- PER: Perform "I Got Rhythms" words and set 1 rhythms in combos of 4.
- PER: "Grand Old Duke" words and pitches, and "following the leader" game.

Activities:

1. "Windmills" coordinating motions with breathing and hissing/humming. (p 5)
2. "Sameer" letting one student lead.
3. Introduce "Re" in body scale. (p 13)
4. Copycat sequences for "Grand Old Duke…" (p 44)
5. Introduce all of rhythm cards set 2.
6. Practice rhythm cards set 1 in combos of 4.
7. "I Got Rhythms" words and set 1 in combos of 4.
8. Read story to "Grand Old Duke."
9. Teach "Grand Old Duke…" words & melody together by rote together.
10. Sing "Grand Old Duke" while playing follow the leader, letting students take turns as leader.

Assignments:

- Practice rhythm cards sets 1 and 2.
- Sing "I've Got Rhythms" with set 1 cards in combos of 4.
- Sing "Grand Old Duke."
- Color Body Scale pictures with correct colors on p 13.

Lesson #8

Objectives: Students will

- TECH: Coordinate posture, belly-breathing, and sustained phrases.
- EAR/RHY: Repeat back copycat sequences.
- SR: Point & say all set 2 cards alone and in combos of 2.
- PER: Perform "I Got Rhythms" words and set 1 rhythms in combos of 4.
- PER: "Grand Old Duke" words and pitches, percussion part, and "following the leader" game.

Activities:

1. "Windmills" coordinating motions with breathing and hissing/humming. (p 5)
2. "Sameer" letting a different student lead.
3. Copycat sequences for "Grand Old Duke…" (p 44)
4. Practice rhythm cards set 2 alone and in combos of 2.
5. "I Got Rhythms" letting students take turn as leader for words part, and set 1 in combos of 4.
6. Teach "Grand Old Duke" with body scale actions.
7. Teach "Grand Old Duke" percussion using point & say. (p 17-18)
8. "Grand Old Duke" with following the leader.

Assignments:

- Practice rhythm cards set 2.
- Sing "I've Got Rhythms" with set 1 cards in combos of 4.
- "Grand Old Duke" with actions, percussion part separately.
- Color "Grand Old Duke" picture. (p 12)

Lesson #9

Objectives: Students will

- TECH: Coordinate posture, belly-breathing, and sustained phrases.
- EAR/RHY: Repeat back copycat sequences.
- SR: Point & say all set 2 cards in combos of 2 and 4.
- PER: "Grand Old Duke" melody, descant, and percussion parts.

- PER: Perform "I Got Rhythms" with set 2 rhythms in combos of 2.

Activities:

1. "Windmills" coordinating motions with breathing and hissing/humming. (p 5)
2. "Sameer" letting a different student lead.
3. Copycat sequences for "Grand Old Duke…" (p 44)
4. Practice rhythm cards set 2 in combos of 2 and 4.
5. Review "Grand Old Duke" percussion with point & say. Then clap/play on rhythm sticks.
6. Teach "Grand Old Duke" descant by rote.
7. Perform "Grand Old Duke," with whole class together switching off between singing words, playing percussion part, and singing descant part.
8. "I Got Rhythms" letting students take turn as leader for words part, and set 2 in combos of 2.

Assignments:

- Practice rhythm cards set 2.
- Sing "I've Got Rhythms" with set 1 cards in combos of 4.
- "Grand Old Duke" melody with actions, descant, and percussion parts separately.

Lesson #10

Objectives: Students will

- TECH: Coordinate posture, belly-breathing, and sustained phrases.
- SR: Point & say all set 1 and 2 cards mixed in combos of 4.
- PER: Perform "I Got Rhythms" with set 1 and 2 rhythms mixed in combos of 4.
- SR: "Melody Reading" and "Grand Old Duke" descant pictorial solfege notation.
- PER: "Grand Old Duke" melody, descant, and percussion parts separately.

Activities:

1. "Windmills" coordinating motions with breathing and hissing/humming. (p 5)
2. "Sameer" letting a different student lead.
3. Practice rhythm cards sets 1 and 2 mixed in combos of 4.
4. "I've Got Rhythms" with sets 1 and 2 in combos of 4.
5. "Melody Reading" using point & sing.
6. Point & sing "Grand Old Duke" descant.
7. Point & say percussion part and then clap or play on sticks/drums.
8. Perform "Grand Old Duke," with whole class together switching off between singing words, playing percussion part, and singing descant part.
9. Read story to "Kumbaya."

Assignments:

- Practice rhythm cards sets 1 and 2 mixed in combos of 4.
- Sing "I've Got Rhythms" with set 1 and 2 cards mixed in combos of 4.
- Practice "Grand Old Duke" descant and percussion parts.
- With adult help, color "Melody Reading" figures with correct colors (p 14). Refer to p 6 and 13 for colors.

Lesson #11

Objectives: Students will

- TECH: Coordinate posture, belly-breathing, and sustained phrases.
- PER: Perform "I Got Rhythms" with set 1 and 2 rhythms mixed in combos of 4.
- SR: "Kumbaya" solfege and "Melody Reading."
- PER: "Grand Old Duke" melody, descant, and percussion parts with students on separate parts.
- PER: "Kumbaya" singing, percussion, and melody solfege separately.

Activities:

1. "Windmills" coordinating motions with breathing and hissing/humming. (p 5)
2. "Sameer" letting a different student lead.
3. "I've Got Rhythms" with sets 1 and 2 in combos of 4.
4. Perform "Grand Old Duke," beginning to have students sing words, play percussion part, and/or sing descant part at the same time.
5. Point & say "Kumbaya" percussion part. (p 22)
6. Point & say "Kumbaya" melody. (p 21)
7. "Melody Reading" using point & sing.
8. Pretend to go camping (see story on p 20) and perform "Kumbaya" with whole class switching off between words, melody solfege, and percussion parts.

Assignments:

- Sing "I've Got Rhythms" with set 1 and 2 cards mixed in combos of 4.

- Practice all "Grand Old Duke" parts.
- Practice "Kumaya" song, melody solfege, and percussion part. Color drawing. (p 20)
- Point and sing "Melody Reading." (p 14)

Lesson #12

Objectives: Students will

- TECH: Coordinate posture, belly-breathing, and sustained phrases.
- PER: Perform "I Got Rhythms" with set 1 and 2 rhythms mixed in combos of 4.
- SR: "Kumbaya" melody and harmony solfege, and percussion.
- PER: "Kumbaya" singing, percussion, harmony and melody solfege separately.
- SR/RHY: Rhythm cards set 3.
- PER: "Kumbaya" singing, percussion, and melody solfege separately.

Activities:

1. "Windmills" coordinating motions with breathing and hissing/humming. (p 5)
2. "Sameer" letting a different student lead.
3. "I've Got Rhythms" with sets 1 and 2 in combos of 4.
4. Point & sing "Kumbaya" melody solfege.
5. See & play "Kumbaya" percussion.
6. Point & sing "Kumbaya" harmony solfege. (p 21)
7. Perform "Kumbaya" with whole class switching off between words, melody solfege, and percussion parts.
8. Introduce rhythm cards set 3.
9. Perform "Grand Old Duke," with students singing words, playing percussion part, and/or singing descant part at the same time.

Assignments:

- Practice rhythm cards set 3.
- Practice all "Grand Old Duke" parts.
- Sight-read and practice all "Kumaya" parts.
- With adult help, color melody and harmony pictorial solfege. (p 21) Refer to p 6 and 13 for colors.

Lesson #13

Objectives: Students will

- TECH: Coordinate posture, belly-breathing, and sustained phrases.
- SR/RHY: Rhythm cards set 3.
- SR: "Kumbaya" melody and harmony solfege, and percussion.
- PER: "Kumbaya" melody and harmony solfege separately and together.
- SR/PER: "Sliver Moonlight" solfege and words.

Activities:

1. "Windmills" coordinating motions with breathing and hissing/humming. (p 5)
2. "Sameer" letting a different student lead.
3. Point & say rhythm cards set 3.
4. Point & sing "Kumbaya" melody solfege.
5. See & play "Kumaya" percussion.
6. Point & sing "Kumbaya" harmony solfege. (p 21)
7. Perform "Kumbaya" with whole class split in two groups: one singing melody solfege and the other the harmony solfege. Sing separately and together.
8. Point & sing "Silver Moonlight." (p 23)
9. Sing "Silver Moonlight" words.

Assignments:

- Practice rhythm cards set 3.
- Practice all "Kumbaya" parts.
- Point & sing "Silver Moonlight." (p 23)
- Practice "Silver Moonlight" with words.
- With adult help, color pictorial solfege. Refer to p 6 and 13 for colors.

Lesson #14

Objectives: Students will

- TECH: Coordinate posture, belly-breathing, and sustained phrases.
- SR/RHY: Rhythm cards set 3.
- SR/PER: "Sliver Moonlight" solfege, and English and French words.
- SR: "Kumbaya" melody and harmony solfege, and percussion.
- PER: "Kumbaya" melody, harmony, and percussion separately and together.

Activities:

1. "Windmills" coordinating motions with breathing and hissing/humming. (p 5)
2. "Sameer" letting a different student lead.
3. Point & say rhythm cards set 3.
4. Point & sing "Silver Moonlight." (p 23)
5. Sing "Silver Moonlight" words.
6. Teach French "Silver Moonlight" words, if desired.

7. Look and sing/play "Kumbaya" melody, harmony, and percussion parts separately.
8. Perform "Kumbaya" with whole class split in two groups: one singing melody solfege and the other the harmony solfege. Sing separately and together.
9. Perform "Kumbaya" with students on melody, harmony, and percussion parts separately and together. (Sing words instead of solfege.)

Assignments:

- Practice rhythm cards set 3.
- Practice all "Kumbaya" parts.
- Point & sing "Silver Moonlight." (p 23)
- Practice "Silver Moonlight" with English and French words.

==

Unit 3:

- TECHNIQUE: Apply basic singing techniques to achieve legato phrasing in songs and exercises.
- EAR TRAINGING: Learn "step down to Ti" step of the Body Scale.
- EAR TRAINING: Become proficient at increasingly difficult melodic and rhythmic sequences.
- SIGHT READING: Read increasingly difficult rhythmic notation and pictorial solfege notation.
- PERFORMANCE: Continue practicing melody and harmony parts sung together.
- PERFORMANCE: Take unique parts in performances combining melody and descant/harmony singing, movement, and percussion parts.

Lesson #15

Objectives: Students will

- TECH: Review posture, belly-breathing, and sustained phrases.
- TECH: Practice crisp consonants and legato vowels.
- PER/SR: "I've Got Rhythms" with all rhythm cards.
- SR/PER: "Silver Moonlight," "Mary Had a Little Lamb," and "Twinkle, Twinkle Little Star" using pictorial solfege notation.
- PER: "Silver Moonlight," "Mary Had a Little Lamb," and "Twinkle, Twinkle Little Star" using words.
- PER: "Kumbaya" melody, harmony, and percussion together.

Activities:

1. "Windmills" coordinating motions with breathing and hissing/humming. (p 5)
2. Read "Sustained Notes Warm-up" story and practice legato "too-too-too"s using motions if desired.
3. Perform "I've Got Rhythms" with mixed sets 1-3 in combos of 4. Let one student lead words.
4. Point & sing "Silver Moonlight." Sing words in English and French.
5. Point & sing "Mary had a Little Lamb." Sing words.
6. Read story to "Twinkle, Twinkle Little Star" and sing V1. Point & sing solfege.
7. Explain how to create extra verses for "Kumbaya."
8. Perform "Kumbaya" with students on melody, harmony, and percussion parts separately and together. (Sing suggested new verse.)

Assignments:

- Point & sing "Silver Moonlight" and "Mary Had a Little Lamb." (p 23)
- With adult help, color pictorial solfege. Refer to p 6 and 13 for colors.
- Point & sing "Twinkle, Twinkle Little Star." (p 26)
- Practice rhythm cards sets 1-3 mixed in combos of 4.
- Practice melody and harmony for "Kumbaya," making up new verses. (p 20)

Lesson #16

Objectives: Students will

- TECH: Review posture, belly-breathing, and sustained phrases.
- TECH: Practice crisp consonants and legato vowels.
- SR/PER: "Mary...Lamb" solfege, words, staccato and legato.
- SR/PER: "Twinkle, Twinkle" solfege, words, and percussion.
- PER: "Kumbaya" melody, harmony, percussion, new verses.

Activities:

1. "Windmills" coordinating motions with breathing and hissing/humming. (p 5)
2. Review "Sustained Notes Warm-up" and practice legato "too-too-too"s using motions if desired.
3. Point & sing "Mary...Lamb" solfege. Sing words.
4. Sing "Mary...Lamb" words staccato and legato. (p 24)
5. Point & sing "Twinkle, Twinkle" solfege. Sing words.

6. Point & say "Twinkle, Twinkle" percussion part. (p 27) Look & play part.
7. Perform "Twinkle, Twinkle" with one group on words and one group saying and playing percussion.
8. Perform "Kumbaya" with students on melody, harmony, and percussion parts. Let one or two students suggest a new verse.

Assignments:

- Practice "Mary…Lamb" words staccato and legato.
- Point & say "Mary…Lamb" and "Twinkle, Twinkle."
- With adult help, color pictorial solfege. Refer to p 6 and 13 for colors.
- Point & say/look & play "Twinkle, Twinkle" percussion part. (p 27)
- Practice melody and harmony for "Kumbaya," making up new verses. (p 20)

Lesson #17

Objectives: Students will

- TECH: Review posture, belly-breathing, and sustained phrases.
- TECH: Practice crisp consonants and legato vowels.
- SR/PER: "Mary…Lamb" and "Twinkle, Twinkle" solfege, words, staccato and legato.
- SR/PER: "Twinkle, Twinkle" solfege, words, percussion, new verses.
- EAR: "Body Scale: Step Down to Ti" and copycat phrases.
- PER: "Kumbaya" melody, harmony, percussion, new verses.

Activities:

1. "Windmills" coordinating motions with breathing and hissing/humming. (p 5)
2. Review "Sustained Notes Warm-up" and practice legato "too-too-too"s using motions if desired.
3. Sing "Mary…Lamb" words staccato and legato. (p 24)
4. Sing "Twinkle, Twinkle" words staccato and legato.
5. Perform "Twinkle…Twinkle" solfege, words, and percussion separately. Sing through each new verse and assign one to each student to memorize. (p27)
6. Teach "Step down to Ti" gestures and copycat phrases. (p 28)
7. Perform "Kumbaya" with students on melody, harmony, and percussion parts. Let one or two students suggest a new verse.

Assignments:

- Point & say "Twinkle, Twinkle" melody and percussion part.
- Practice assigned new verse.
- Color "Step down to Ti" drawing as described.
- Point & say copycat phrases on p 28.
- With adult help, color pictorial solfege. Refer to p 6 and 13 for colors.

Lesson #18

Objectives: Students will

- TECH: Review posture, belly-breathing, and sustained phrases.
- TECH: Practice crisp consonants and legato vowels.
- SR/PER: "Twinkle, Twinkle" solfege, words (staccato and legato) percussion, and assigned verses.
- EAR: "Body Scale: Step Down to Ti" and copycat phrases.
- SR/PER: "Go to the Circus" solfege and percussion.
- PER: "Kumbaya" melody, harmony, percussion, new verses.

Activities:

1. "Windmills" coordinating motions with breathing and hissing/humming. (p 5)
2. Review "Sustained Notes Warm-up" and practice legato "too-too-too"s using motions if desired.
3. Sing "Twinkle, Twinkle" words staccato and legato.
4. Perform "Twinkle…Twinkle" solfege, words, and percussion separately. Let each student lead their own assigned verse.
5. Review "Step down to Ti" and begin practicing melodic and rhythmic sequences on p 45.
6. Read story to "Go to the Circus." (p30)
7. Point & say solfege (p 30) and percussion. (p 31)
8. Perform "Kumbaya" with students on melody, harmony, and percussion parts. Let one or two students suggest a new verse.

Assignments:

- Point & say "Go to the Circus" solfege (p 30) and percussion part. (p31)
- With adult help, color pictorial solfege. Refer to p 6, 13, and 32 for colors.
- Complete 8th note beams on p 31.
- Practice "Twinkle, Twinkle" melody, percussion, and new assigned verse.

Lesson #19

Objectives: Students will

- TECH: Review posture, belly-breathing, and sustained phrases.
- TECH: Practice crisp consonants and legato vowels.
- PER: "Silver Moonlight" words staccato and legato.
- EAR: Copycat phrases.
- SR/PER: "Go to the Circus" solfege, percussion, and words.
- SR/PER: "Twinkle, Twinkle" words and percussion, and assigned verses.

Activities:

1. "Windmills" coordinating motions with breathing and hissing/humming. (p 5)
2. Review "Sustained Notes Warm-up" and practice legato "too-too-too"s using motions if desired.
3. Sing "Silver Moonlight" words staccato and legato.
4. Copycat sequences. (p 45)
5. Point & say "Circus" percussion.
6. Point & sing "Circus" solfege.
7. Teach words by rote (with gestures, if desired).
8. Perform "Twinkle…Twinkle" words and percussion together. Let each student lead their own assigned verse.

Assignments:

- Point & sing/play "Go to the Circus" solfege and percussion.
- Practice "Circus" melody and words.
- Practice "Twinkle, Twinkle" melody, percussion, and new assigned verse.

==

Unit 4:

- TECHNIQUE: Apply basic singing techniques to achieve legato phrasing in songs and exercises.
- EAR TRAINGING: Learn "Jump down to So" in the Body Scale.
- EAR TRAINING: Become proficient at increasingly difficult melodic and rhythmic sequences.
- SIGHT READING: Read increasingly difficult rhythmic notation and pictorial solfege notation.
- PERFORMANCE: Continue practicing melody and harmony parts sung together.
- PERFORMANCE: Take unique parts in performances combining melody and descant/harmony singing, movement, and percussion parts.
- TECHNIQUE: Learn very basic piano technique in order to play songs on piano.
- Solidify skills acquired in level and demonstrate readiness for Level C.

Lesson #20

Objectives: Students will

- TECH: Review posture, belly-breathing, and sustained phrases.
- TECH: Practice crisp consonants and legato vowels.
- PER/SR: "Circus" words (staccato/legato), solfege, percussion, actions.
- TECH: "Jump down to So" body scale and copycat.
- SR/PER: "Twinkle, Twinkle" words and percussion, and assigned verses.

Activities:

1. "Windmills" coordinating motions with breathing and hissing/humming. (p 5)
2. Review "Sustained Notes Warm-up" and practice legato "too-too-too"s using motions if desired.
3. Speak and sing "Circus" words staccato and legato. Perform while students all act as clowns.
4. Point & say/sing "Circus" solfege and percussion.
5. Teach "Jump down to So" and copycat phrases. (p 32)
6. Copycat sequences. (p 45)
7. Perform "Twinkle…Twinkle" words and percussion together. Let each student lead their own assigned verse.

Assignments:

- Point & sing/play "Go to the Circus" solfege and percussion.
- Practice "Circus" melody and words while acting out different circus performers.
- Practice "Jump down to So" copycat sequences on p 32.
- Color "Jump down to So" drawing as described.

Lesson #21

Objectives: Students will

- TECH: Review posture, belly-breathing, and sustained phrases.
- TECH: Practice crisp consonants and legato vowels.
- PER: "Kumbaya" words (staccato/legato).
- TECH: Copycat sequences.
- SR/PER: "Frere Jacques" solfege, words, ostinato.
- PER: "Circus" words, solfege, percussion, actions.

Activities:

1. "Windmills" coordinating motions with breathing and hissing/humming. (p 5)
2. Review "Sustained Notes Warm-up" story and practice legato "too-too-too"s using motions if desired.
3. Speak and sing "Kumbaya" words staccato and legato. Perform with melody and harmony parts.
4. Copycat sequences. (p 45)
5. Point & sing solfege "Frere Jacques" (p 34)
6. Teach English words by rote.
7. One group repeats ostinato "Ding Dong Ding" while second point & sings melody.
8. Perform "Circus" with different students on melody and percussion. Perform while students all act like different performers. (see p 29)

Assignments:

- Point & sing "Frere Jacques" solfege and sing English words.
- With adult help, color pictorial solfege. Refer to p 6, 13, and 32 for colors.
- Practice "Circus" melody and words while acting out different circus performers.

Lesson #22

Objectives: Students will

- TECH: Review posture, belly-breathing, and sustained phrases.
- TECH: Practice crisp consonants and legato vowels.
- PER: "Grand Old Duke" melody (staccato/legato), descant, and percussion parts with actions.
- EAR: Copycat sequences.
- SR/PER: "Frere Jacques" solfege, words (English/French), piano.
- PER: "Circus" words, solfege, percussion, actions.

Activities:

1. "Windmills" coordinating motions with breathing and hissing/humming. (p 5)
2. Review "Sustained Notes Warm-up" story and practice legato "too-too-too"s using motions if desired.
3. Speak and sing "Grand Old Duke" words staccato and legato. Perform with melody, descant, and percussion parts and actions.
4. Copycat sequences. (p 45)
5. Sing "Frere Jacques" in English.
6. Point & sing solfege "Frere Jacques."
7. Teach first 2 lines of "Frere Jacques" on piano. (p 35)
8. Teach French words by rote.
9. Perform "Circus" with different students on melody and percussion. Perform while students all act like different performers. (see p 29)

Assignments:

- Point & sing "Frere Jacques" solfege.
- Practice English and French words. (p 33)
- Practice first 2 lines of piano part. (p 35)
- Color picture on p 35.

Lesson #23

Objectives: Students will

- TECH: Review posture, belly-breathing, and sustained phrases.
- TECH: Practice crisp consonants and legato vowels.
- PER: "I've Got Rhythms" melody (staccato/legato), and rhythm cards.
- EAR: Copycat sequences.
- SR/PER: "Frere Jacques" solfege, words (English/French), piano.
- PER: "Circus" words, solfege, percussion, actions.

Activities:

1. "Windmills" coordinating motions with breathing and hissing/humming. (p 5)
2. Review "Sustained Notes Warm-up" story and practice legato "too-too-too"s using motions if desired.
3. Speak and sing "I've Got Rhythms" words staccato and legato. Perform with mixed rhythm cards sets 1-3 in combos of 4.
4. Sing "Frere Jacques" in English and French.
5. Point & sing solfege "Frere Jacques."
6. Review first 2 lines on piano and teach the remainder.

7. Perform "Circus" with different students on melody and percussion. Perform while students all act like different performers. (see p 29)

Assignments:

- Point & sing "Frere Jacques" solfege.
- Practice English and French words. (p 33)
- Practice piano part. (p 35)

Lesson #24

Objectives: Students will

- TECH: Review posture, belly-breathing, and sustained phrases.
- TECH: Practice crisp consonants and legato vowels.
- PER/SR: "Frere Jacques" words English (staccato/legato) and French, solfege, piano.
- RHY: "Gallop" rhythm.
- PER: "Gallop" melody with words and game.

Activities:

1. "Windmills" coordinating motions with breathing and hissing/humming. (p 5)
2. Review "Sustained Notes Warm-up" story and practice legato "too-too-too"s using motions if desired.
3. Speak and sing "Frere Jacques" words staccato and legato in English.
4. Review "Frere Jacques" French words.
5. Point & sing solfege. Review on piano.
6. Teach "Gallop" percussion. (p 36)
7. Teach "Gallop" melody and words by rote.
8. Teach "Gallop" game. (see p 36 on bottom)

Assignments:

- Practice "Frere Jacques" in English and French and on piano.
- Practice "Gallop" percussion and melody with words.
- Color "Gallop" picture. (p 36)

Lesson #25

Objectives: Students will

- TECH: Review posture, belly-breathing, and sustained phrases.
- TECH: Practice crisp consonants and legato vowels.
- PER/SR: "Frere Jacques" words English and French (staccato/legato), solfege, piano.
- PER/RHY: "A-Hunting We Will Go" words and rhythm.
- SR/PER: "Gallop" solfege, words and game.

Activities:

1. "Windmills" coordinating motions with breathing and hissing/humming. (p 5)
2. Review "Sustained Notes Warm-up" story and practice legato "too-too-too"s using motions if desired.
3. Speak and sing "Frere Jacques" words staccato and legato in French.
4. Review "Gallop" percussion.
5. Chant "A-Hunting We Will Go" words to "Gallop" rhythm.
6. Teach "A-Hunting" melody and words by rote.
7. Perform "Gallop" melody and words with percussion.
8. Point & sing "Gallop" solfege.
9. Sing and play "Gallop" game.

Assignments:

- Practice "Frere Jacques" in English and French and on piano.
- Practice "Gallop" percussion and song.
- Point & say "Gallop" and "Frere Jacques" solfege.
- Practice "A-Hunting" melody and words. (p 38)

Lesson #26

Objectives: Students will

- TECH: Review posture, belly-breathing, and sustained phrases.
- TECH: Practice crisp consonants and legato vowels.
- PER/SR: "A-Hunting" words (staccato/legato), solfege, and game.
- SR/PER: "Gallop" solfege, words and game.

Activities:

1. "Windmills" coordinating motions with breathing and hissing/humming. (p 5)
2. Review "Sustained Notes Warm-up" story and practice legato "too-too-too"s using motions if desired.
3. Speak and sing "A-Hunting" words staccato and legato.
4. Point & say "A-Hunting" solfege.

5. Teach "A-Hunting" game. (see bottom of p 37)
6. Point & say "Gallop" percussion and solfege.
7. Perform "Gallop" with game.

Assignments:

- Point & say "Gallop" and "A-Hunting" solfege.
- Practice "Gallop" and "A-Hunting."
- Practice "Frere Jacques" in English and French and on piano.
- Color "A-Hunting" picture. (p 38)
- Practice all rhythm cards.

Lesson #27

Objectives:

The Teacher will

- Observe student readiness to pass level. (Use assessment on p 39.) Reteach or work with students as needed.
- Choose songs to be performed in last lesson in 2 weeks. (Recommended: "I've Got Rhythms" with rhythm cards, "Kumbaya" with harmony and new verses, "Twinkle, Twinkle" with solo verses, "Circus" with actions, "Frere Jacques" in French and English and any students ready to do piano (probably separately, at their own speed), "Gallop" with game, "A-Hunting" with game, and any more that are ready and that you have time to do.

Students will

- TECH: Review posture, belly-breathing, and sustained phrases.
- PER/TECH: "Sameer" with body scale gestures.
- PER/RHY: "Grand Old Duke" with descant and percussion.
- PER/EAR: "Kumbaya" with melody and harmony.
- PER: "Gallop" and "A-Hunting" with game.

Activities:

1. "Windmills" coordinating motions with breathing and hissing/humming. (p 5)
2. Perform/Rehearse "Sameer" with all body scale actions.
3. Perform/Rehearse "I've Got Rhythms" with mixed rhythm cards in combos of 4.
4. Perform/Rehearse "Grand Old Duke" with actions, descant, and percussion parts.
5. Perform/Rehearse "Kumbaya" with melody and harmony parts solfege and with words.

6. Perform "Gallop" and "A-Hunting" with game.

Assignments:

- Practice "Frere Jacques" in English and French and on piano.
- Point and say "Twinkle, Twinkle," and "Go to the Circus."
- (Assign songs to practice that you plan on performing in the final lesson the week after next.)

Lesson #28

Objectives:

The Teacher will

- Observe student readiness to pass level. (Use assessment on p 39.) Reteach or work with students as needed.

Students will

- TECH: Review posture, belly-breathing, and sustained phrases.
- PER/SR: "Silver Moonlight" solfege, and words English and French.
- PER/SR: "Mary...Lamb" solfege and words.
- PER/SR: "Twinkle, Twinkle" solfege, words, percussion, and individual verses.
- PER/SR: "Circus" solfege, words, percussion
- PER/TECH: "Frere Jacques" solfege, words (English and French) and piano.
- PER: "Gallop" and "A-Hunting" and games.

Activities:

1. "Windmills" coordinating motions with breathing and hissing/humming. (p 5)
2. Perform/Rehearse "Silver Moonlight" solfege (point and say, if necessary) and words, English and French.
3. Perform/Rehearse "Mary...Lamb" solfege and words.
4. Perform/Rehearse "Twinkle, Twinkle" solfege, words, percussion, and individual verses.
5. Perform/Rehearse "Circus" solfege, words, and percussion.
6. Perform/Rehearse "Frere Jacques" solfege, words (English and French) and piano.
7. Perform "Gallop" and "A-Hunting" games.
8. Ask parents to prepare for recital next week. (Bring treats, cameras, etc.)

Assignments:

- Practice songs to be performed in recital next week.
- Bring treats, cameras, etc. for recital next week.

Lesson #29

Objectives:

The Teacher will

- Make students and parents feel a sense of accomplishment for completing level.
- Encourage students and parents to continue with you on to Level C.

Students will

- TECH: Demonstrate mastery of vocal, percussion, and piano techniques taught in Level B.
- EAR/RHY/SR: Demonstrate mastery of solfege, rhythm, and derivative sequences taught in Level B.
- PER: Demonstrate mastery of songs taught in Level B, and ability to take part in group and with solo percussion, descant, harmony, etc. parts.

Activities:

1. Welcome parents to final class, congratulate students, thank students and parents for all their hard work, explain that today the children will show all of the new talents that they learned in Level B.
2. Invite parents and students to new Level C by talking about some of the new things they will be doing.
3. Perform the various numbers you have been rehearsing. (It is suggested that you perform as many of them that are in a good enough state to perform. Also, allow time for students to perform "Frere Jacques" on piano, if desired.)
4. Sign and hand out certificates. (p 40 and on website)
5. Refreshments and visiting.

Printed in Great Britain
by Amazon